"There is an ancient proverb, 'When the student is ready the teacher appears.' By reading this book you will see intimately that this is exactly the story of Jason Garner, a person ready to master the lessons of life. Not only is this book one of wonderful free-form instruction, but it is a book of great humor—for without this lighter element there is no way to truly learn, to overcome, or to move forward…lessons without light are a complete drag.

I highly recommend Jason's stories to everyone who has a goal, a plan, a challenge and a destiny to achieve the ordinary, or perhaps even the extraordinary. … *And I Breathed* is a blueprint for unleashing great success out of the improbable—and sometimes, the impossible."

—**Guru Singh**, third-generation yogi and master teacher of Humanology and Kundalini (yoga, meditation and mantra). He is also a musician, composer, and author of five books, including his latest: *Buried Treasures: The Journey from Where You Are to Who You Are.*

"Beautiful, poignant and deep! I loved this book as it touched me on many levels. Jason Garner is refreshingly open and honest with his emotions, which makes this book such a breath of fresh air!"

—**Anita Moorjani**, *New York Times* best-selling author of the book, *Dying to be Me*, and internationally renowned speaker

"We are all like seeds planted in the earth. But without nourishment we cannot reach our full potential. Jason is one of those beings who, like the sun and the rain, imparts wisdom and love to help people grow."

Bo

"For years I had the pleasure of working with ⎯⎯⎯⎯⎯⎯⎯⎯⎯ ⎯⎯⎯ment executive. Through his blog and this book, I now have the ⎯⎯⎯ ⎯⎯ing inspired by the writings of Jason, the awakened man. Jason combines business expertise, spiritual teachings, and real-world sensibility in providing tools everyone can use in finding balance in their busy lives. Jason's insights make finding true peace and joy accessible to us all—right from the desks where we are sitting."

—**Luis Balaguer**, Co-founder with Sofia Vergara of Latin World Entertainment

"Stripped naked, Jason unveils his heart with profound courage and relentless self honesty. Through laughter and tears, his journey 'home' both humbled and challenged me. I couldn't put it down. This is a book I will cherish and read often."

—**Anne Mejia**, Co-founder Best Friends Animal Society

"I have been an editor for 30 years and have crafted many a sentence for others. But never before have I 'lived' a book as I did with ... *And I Breathed*. With his words and his wisdom, Jason Garner reached into this editor's often jaded soul. His lessons transform the reader: he does not lecture, he guides, sharing what he has been blessed to learn with those who need a gentle push into self-exploration and, ultimately, into a delightful awakening of the human spirit."

—**Kathleen Yasas**, Editor, ... *And I Breathed*

"This book is a profound and unequalled memoir filled with real-life lessons in the unbelievable journey of Jason Garner, who went from flea market entrepreneur to executive to spiritual student. While this is Jason's story, it represents, in a larger sense, the lives of all of us who have sought the balance between our careers and spirituality. I read this book three times and I cried each time as Jason's adventures and honest teachings touched and inspired me. This book caused me to reflect on my own life, and awakened a spiritual energy that has been locked inside me for many years. We need Jason Garner to keep writing and sharing."

—**Joe Heitzler**, Chairman/CEO of Entertainment Management Group, former Chairman/CEO of CART Racing, and former President of Forum Sports and Entertainment (Los Angeles Lakers, Clippers, and Kings)

"With unflinching and uncompromising bravery, Jason uncovers his life story with all of the emotions and beliefs attached to it. One by one, he begins to unwind the Gordian knots that bound him inextricably to his past, and that caused him to repeat the very same patterns in his current life that kept him anchored to the blueprint of his childhood behavior. His journey toward light, life, and ultimate fulfillment of self is unique to him, but also so universal that others can readily see themselves in Jason's search for a life of love, purpose, and passion.

I defy anyone to read this book and not be moved to tears, or become inspired to examine and transform their own life."

—**Beverly Kitaen Morse, Ph.D.**, Executive Director, Integrative Body Psychotherapy Training Institute, Co-author of *The Intimate Couple* with Jack Rosenberg, Ph.D.

...AND I
Breathed

MY JOURNEY FROM A LIFE OF MATTER
TO A LIFE THAT MATTERS

JASON GARNER

TO MY MOM

FOREWORD

THE HERO'S JOURNEY

... AND I BREATHED IS THE SELF-TOLD STORY OF JASON GARNER, THE MAN who chased the American Dream and found it, only to realize the dream was the preamble to a greater, deeper, and more profound examination of the human condition.

From his origins as an impoverished child living with his single mom in the dusty Arizona desert, Jason rose to become one of the top 20 highest paid executives in the country under 40 years old, as recognized by *Fortune* magazine. Jason's journey from hungry street kid to dining with President Obama and socializing with rock stars is the substance of fairy tales and fantasies.

Jason's story of his corporate ascension is an exciting, page-turning read. For most of his life, Jason climbed the ladder of success, running away from the fears and insecurities of his childhood programming. The higher up the ladder Jason climbed the more frightened, exhausted, and stressed out he became as his life was overshadowed by his fear of failure.

Like so many others who have attained power and riches, Jason's success did not lead to inner peace. The core of Jason's awakening began at age 37, when his mother died suddenly and he walked away from the corporate world, causing him to jump into the abyss on his quest for personal transformation.

Jason's story is the heart of modern mythology, a tale offering timeless truths that point the way to our ultimate destiny. The pursuit of that destiny is reflected in the three phases of Joseph Campbell's *The Hero's Journey*: Separation, Initiation and Return. In Jason's hero's journey, *Separation* was his rise from trailer park to corporate executive; *Initiation* was represented in his leaving of the corporate world in search of finding his true self as he traveled the world meeting gurus, monks, scientists, and kung fu masters. Finally, we see Jason *Return* in his real-life application of all he has learned on his journey and the sharing of it through this book ... our hero has found his calling.

Jason's transformation results in an understanding of life's essence and its ultimate purpose: finding love ... especially love of self ... and then achieving a state of selflessness and an ability to experience unconditional love.

By expanding his consciousness, Jason realizes there is an indestructible life beyond the physical body. Leaving the mystical world and returning to "regular" life, he is able to bring the knowledge of his adventure home to share with others.

I wholeheartedly believe Jason Garner has succeeded admirably at this hero's task. *... And I Breathed* is an inspiring story, aligning readers with

Jason's journey in a way that goes beyond the printed word and impacts the reader's own life.

Filled with great depth of insight and understanding, Jason's anthology of personal and intimate experiences offers empowering insights that free us from self-sabotaging emotions. When applied, his insights will dramatically accelerate the expression of our true nature as spiritual beings of unlimited potential.

Jason Garner's essays—told in breezy yet profound prose—offer the hope of enlightenment, peace, and harmony...for ourselves...and, indeed, for our world.

Bruce H. Lipton, Ph.D., is a cell biologist and bestselling author of *The Biology of Belief: Unleashing the Power of Consciousness, Matter and Miracles; The Honeymoon Effect: The Science of Creating Heaven on Earth*; and coauthor of *Spontaneous Evolution: Our Positive Future (And A Way To Get There From Here)*.

PREFACE

FOR AS LONG AS I CAN REMEMBER MY FRIENDS HAVE BEEN TELLING ME, "Someday you have to write a book." But I never wanted to write the book they were talking about, the one men write as a last-ditch effort to get applause for their life's accomplishments.

In my case that would have been the one-in-a-million story of a poor boy, raised by a single mom, who goes on to become the confidant of stars of the music, sports, and business worlds. See what I mean? It's just so gratuitously arrogant, and it's not me.

Then something happened. The story changed. And in what seemed like the blink of an eye my life turned upside down and the myth of Jason, the superstar, was shifted and changed forever.

So I decided to take a left turn. I gave myself a break. I took a time out. I began a journey to know myself and, in the process, I learned a great deal about others, too.

Soon my friends, noticing positive changes in me, began to say it again: "You should write a book." At first my reaction was the same as it had always been—a smile, a shrug, and a polite "Nah, that's not for me."

But as I gave it more thought I began to visualize a book I could write, in fact one I should write—a tell-all book, not one that dished secrets about others, but the true story about what, on my journey, I learned about my own inner workings and, by extension, about us all.

With the encouragement of my wife, Christy, and my friend, Brad Kava, I sat down one afternoon in my bedroom with my laptop and began to write. What happened next surprised everybody, including me. I wrote and wrote and wrote. In fact for 14 days and nights I did nothing but write. It was as though my fingers were responding to something deep inside me, a story, or stories, that just needed to be released.

When I finished I had written what you are about to read—26 essays about my life. This is not a polished beginning, middle, and end book written by a public relations specialist. It is, instead, a raw compilation of the stories that poured from me over that two-week period. It's honest and real, the true stories of my drive to the top, my innermost doubts and fears once I arrived, my devastation at the loss of my mom, and how I finally learned to breathe.

It's my hope that you find some value in these stories, that they serve as a loving friend on your own adventure through life. If these stories touch you please share them with others who might find solace, a laugh, or an understanding from them.

Big hugs of love and gratitude,

·1·

MY MYTH

I WOKE UP IN THE MIDDLE OF THE NIGHT IN A COLD SWEAT, PANICKED, my heart pounding and my mind racing. I had been scared before but this was different. There was no work to hide behind, nothing to comfort me.

After spending a lifetime defining myself with one success after another, rising from a job parking cars in a dirt parking lot at the flea market to becoming CEO of Global Music at Live Nation—the world's largest concert promoter—I was unemployed.

At 37 I was twice divorced, the single father of two children. My mom had recently died and I no longer had my job. Not just any job, but *the* job, the one that had been my calling card for over a decade. I was a concert promoter, an important one. Or so I thought.

I lay in bed trembling, a lifetime of accomplishments silenced by the voice in my head screaming, "YOU'RE SCREWED NOW, JASON." I was always afraid this was coming; the voice in my head had haunted me with messages of doom and gloom my entire life, provoking a fear that had pushed me higher and higher looking for a reprieve. But at each milestone the voice taunted me: "That's not good enough, Jason. You have to do more." And so I did. Over and over again I defied the odds and won, believing that with each success I would find peace and somehow quiet the voice, but still it tortured me.

So many of my dreams had come true, the things I used to dream about when I was a kid living in a trailer with my single mom in the Arizona desert. Yet with each new dream fulfilled came new and more powerful doubts. It was as if each time I did something great the universe rewarded me with an ever-growing monkey on my back, a monkey made up of all the fears and insecurities I had collected during a rocket-like rise from poverty to the proverbial top.

- After starting my career booking Spanish-language performers at a rodeo on weekends, I'd ascended the ranks of the music industry to become one of the top concert promoters in the world.
- I'd helped promote the tours of thousands of artists, including Coldplay, John Mayer, Shakira, Nickelback, Beyoncé, Maroon 5, Enrique Iglesias, and Jay-Z.
- Despite barely finishing high school, I was named to *Fortune* magazine's list of the top 20 highest paid executives in the country under 40 years old. Twice.

I'd even had dinner with President Obama at George Clooney's house as part of the largest fundraiser in the history of presidential politics.

I should have been happy, ecstatic, right? And I was, kind of, but I didn't feel loved. I was trembling inside. I had always been afraid of failure, but the more money I made, the more I had to lose. The closer I got to the top the more the fear turned to terror. There was an ever-increasing feeling that something bad was going to happen to take away everything I'd earned. I had moments of happiness of course, hanging with rock stars and being the boss, but inside I was slowly falling apart—stressed out, exhausted, scared.

When I woke up that day with no job and no fancy title to mask the feelings, I was forced to stare head on at my life and realize that I had no idea who I was. I knew what I had done, but I didn't know me.

So I went on a quest to answer the question: "What do I have to do to FEEL successful?"

I found some of the greatest teachers in the world and spent thousands of hours studying with them. I even went to the mountains of China, to the Shaolin Temple, trying to find the inner peace that had eluded me despite so much success.

That's why I wrote this book: to share what I found on my journey.

I believe you can have happiness and money. You can have fun and be spiritual. You can care about the world and still care for yourself. You can say fuck and shit and scratch your balls and still be enlightened. And you can change the world from your desk at work as easily as a guru can from an ashram.

So here's the deal. If you read on, I can promise you some stories of the hard-earned lessons I learned, raw honesty you won't find anywhere else, spiced with enough rock 'n' roll to keep you turning the pages.

·2·

MY FATHER WAS AN ASSHOLE

MY FATHER WAS AN ASSHOLE. I KNOW THERE ARE MORE SPIRITUALLY correct and sensitive ways to say it, but that's not how I feel. And when you hear about Earl Robert Garner, you'll probably want to use the same word.

I don't have many memories of my dad. He left us when I was three years old. He came back a few times for a day or two as if to rub salt in the wounds of his fatherless children, and then he'd leave again. My relatives described him to me as a con man and a hustler. Perhaps the most telling story of who my dad was goes like this:

His sister had severe autism and attended a special school. His mother saved up relentlessly to pay the bills and one day was about to drive to school to pay his sister's monthly tuition. My father, who had just returned from one of his many sabbaticals from mainstream life, gave his mother the puppy-dog eyes and told her how much he cared and how he'd like to help her out by bringing the money down to the school office for her. She gave it to him and that was the last they saw of him or the money, until he found himself broke again.

See what I mean? *Asshole.*

But I have to admit, I've learned too much to say I'm not like my dad. I got something from my father. Some DNA, of course, and some programming that helped me survive as I hustled and fought my way from the bottom of the economic dog pile.

I do have to give some credit to the man I spent most of my life hating, or just forgetting. He gave me the coldness I needed to survive in a business that routinely chews people up and spits them out. This was tempered by the values of love and compassion I got from my mother.

This unlikely combination of characteristics made me who I am—a blend of the ruthless, shark-like qualities of my father and the open, loving, and insecure nature of my mother. They were two alien, opposing figures, stretching my mind like Silly Putty and shaping someone I wouldn't understand for another 40 years.

It's the same for us all. Our DNA and our environment molding our infant brains, creating a story of who we think we are. This story becomes our truth, our own personalized reality. And through it we are destined to replay the stories of our parents. Or not. But that comes later in this book.

For now, I had one thing in my young reality that became a driving force: we were broke. We never had enough money. This scared me and I knew from a young age that I had to do something about it. I had to find a way to rise above it.

One of my earliest memories was of being bused to middle school in the wealthy suburb of Los Gatos, California. We qualified for subsidized lunches, but there was no way I was going to be the kid who had to get in line for the free lunch.

I saw a kid selling candy in school one day and had an idea. I convinced my mother to drop me off on the corner near the school and I took a quarter and bought a pack of gum from the nearby 7-Eleven. Then I sold the five pieces of gum to my friends for a quarter each.

I used the profits to pay for my lunch and repeated the process every day that school year. I realized in that one moment, standing in the schoolyard discreetly hawking gum, that I had the power to change the Garner Family story of never having enough money and living at the mercy of others. From that day forward, my eyes would always be peeled for a chance to make a buck to free myself from the limits of lack.

When you grow up with no dad and no money, the odds are stacked against you. Everywhere you look—your family, your friends, TV, movies—the stories all say you won't make it. So you learn quickly that you have to question them all. "Why not?" and "You can't tell me what to do!" become your best friends. Because without a stubborn refusal to accept the limitations of the current story, you'll never break through.

That was my first lesson: I had the power to make money. I could change my family story.

·3·

THE FLEA MARKET, TIRE TACKS, AND THE ICE CREAM TRUCK

WHEN I WAS IN HIGH SCHOOL, SAN JOSE HAD TWO FLEA MARKETS. ONE of them, the Berryessa market, brought in four million visitors a year and was listed in the top ten California tourist attractions, behind Disneyland and Hearst Castle.

I worked at the smaller Capitol Flea Market, 1,000 vendors and 10,000 shoppers three times a week in the city that provided cheap labor for Silicon Valley's high-tech companies. Secretaries, factory line workers, janitors, bus boys, drivers, haulers, lifters, painters ... they all lived in San Jose and drove up Highway 101 to work at places like Hewlett Packard, Apple, and Sun Microsystems, or to work as domestic help for the new tech millionaires.

For most people the flea market was a bustling marketplace filled with new immigrants looking for a bargain. But for me it was high school, college, and grad school wrapped into one old, dirty, dusty drive-in movie theater.

Over time I would ascend the ranks and eventually run the whole operation, but for now I was 16, wearing an orange shirt and spending my day as a parking attendant. I was one of a dozen or so teenage workers who directed thousands and thousands of people, most of whom spoke only Spanish, into their parking places. They must have all wondered what this blonde-haired, blue-eyed gringo was doing there.

My flea market job was a continuation of the lesson I'd learned in grade school: you could make money selling stuff. Only here there wasn't just bubble gum. It was a smorgasbord of commerce spread out on blankets and spilling out of boxes filled with everything from shampoo bottles to T-shirts to power tools.

The characters I met fascinated me as I learned the ropes of this underground economy. People like Mr. Calderon, who sold reconditioned tires. These are tires that were once worn down, but now had been retreaded and could be purchased for half of what a new tire cost. Mr. Calderon looked like an Hispanic Mr. Goodwrench and walked the flea market each morning wearing blue coveralls, hand-in-hand with his small son. This touched me as I imagined what it would have been like to have a dad who walked with me. Or at least that was *my* version of the story.

Mr. Calderon had a much different agenda. You see, as they walked, his cute little boy would drop tacks on the ground—tacks that would eventually wind up in someone's tire. At the end of flea market day, some poor soul would appear at Mr. Calderon's booth buying one of his recycled tires. He was literally creating customers as he walked!

Or Linda the single mom, who had emigrated from the Philippines. She sold car seat covers. You remember those—you could upgrade your car's interior with a choice of tiger stripes, faux lamb's wool, or the logo of your favorite football team. Linda, all alone and looking for some special attention, knew two things: young men like food and beautiful women. So she and her sexy daughter (whose name I can't remember because I was too bashful to talk to the girl in the crop-top and Daisy Dukes) would cook lunch for all of us hungry teenagers. In exchange we looked the other way when she took extra space for her goods, and kept out a special eye to make sure that no one messed with them.

Terry was one of my first entrepreneurial mentors, the flea market's version of a rock star. He was different from most of the other vendors. He had blonde hair and blue eyes and was born to a rich father who expected him to work, which he wasn't much inclined to do. So he found an easy solution. He had the nicest trailer truck at the flea market, which his father had surely bought him. During the week he would attend an auction or two until he had filled that truck with whatever treasures he thought would sell. After an evening on the town, he would show up late at the flea market, often with a new woman with whom he'd spent the night. He'd buy five or six spaces and spread his items out. Not nicely displayed, but heaped in boxes. His strategy was simple and born from laziness, like his life—"stack 'em high and watch 'em buy."

The king of the sellers was Produce John. He was a tall, lanky man from Greece who looked like he had just stepped off a tractor. Produce John had mastered the art of selling. Unlike Terry, John worked hard. He had multiple booths, appearing to compete with himself; in reality he was helping to create the marketplace he dominated. His was the closest thing to a farmer's market in those days—table after table heaped with fresh fruits and vegetables. His strategy was one that every great retail operation masters: "location, location, location."

Here I was in this ocean of opportunity, a secret city hidden within a city. While my co-workers were toiling away parking cars and counting the minutes before they could go home, I was in entrepreneurial heaven. Everywhere I looked people were buying stuff. They were buying and selling anything and everything. All I needed to do now was find some stuff to sell.

The flea market was a weekend job, so on school days I worked in the evenings at a different kind of market, Target. One day while stocking the shelves I found what I'd been looking for, something really cheap to sell at the flea market: a bunch of English/Spanish dictionaries marked down on clearance to ten cents each. I bought 50 of them for five dollars and began to imagine the mini fortune I would make.

The next week I showed up at the market, which really looked like old Mexico, walked up to people and showed them the books.

"Do you want to learn English?" I'd ask. "If you want to learn English, you have to have this book." They couldn't buy them fast enough. I sold out in a day, at five dollars each, and had the most money I'd ever seen in my life. I quit my job at Target and focused on one thing—finding more ways to make money at the flea market.

Now it was just a matter of finding more things to sell at higher prices. I borrowed $900 from a friend and bought an old Toyota pickup at auction, like I'd seen other vendors do. I fixed it up and sold it for twice what I paid for it.

Then I bought an ice cream truck. Yes, an ice cream truck, one I got for a steal from a guy who really needed money. I thought buying the truck was a genius move. This was something I could really make some money on. But when I got it home, I found out the refrigeration compressor was broken and it would cost more to fix than I could sell it for. Now I had an ice cream truck that wouldn't freeze ice cream. Too stubborn to admit I'd been duped, I turned it into a positive and used the truck to haul goods to the market. I would drive the truck in and pay someone to sell stuff while I did my job parking cars.

I found a store going out of business that was selling soccer cleats for next to nothing. Boxes and boxes of them. I bought them all and loaded up my truck, where the ice cream would have gone.

Soccer wasn't that big for Americans yet. But who loved it? The Mexican shoppers at the flea market, of course. I made a killing on the shoes, bringing just the right item to market. Sure, someone else could have done that, but they didn't. They were focused on the people who came into their big fancy box stores but had no clue about the under market of new immigrants who wanted to shop the way they did in their old country and didn't have the money to pay what stores needed for their overhead.

That truck became my best friend. I bought and sold and hauled everything from roses to entire estate sales; and while it was all about making money at the time, I was slowly reprogramming my mind from poverty to opportunity, from lack to abundance, and from living at the whim of my circumstance to creating something new.

This would be my next great lesson: that opportunity is everywhere. You just have to look for it.

· 4 ·

EL BUKI, BOLIVIA, AND THE BOXER

IN SCHOOL I LEARNED ABOUT THE IMMIGRANTS WHO FOUNDED THIS country. At the time it was just another story in a history book I was forced to read. But like all stories, there are many perspectives. At the flea market I began to learn a much more personal perspective by talking with the largely Mexican population of vendors. This is how I learned to speak Spanish.

It began innocently, with my asking how to say this or that. The more I asked, the more they wanted to talk to me. Soon I became entrenched in the beautiful cadence and rhythm of the language.

Spanish came easily to me. I almost want to say that something in a past life must have made it so, but I won't get that airy-fairy this early in the book and scare you away, so I'll save that 'til later! For now I'll just say I had a love affair with Spanish and, like most true love affairs, parts of it are beyond explanation.

These new friends were my teachers, my guides to a romantic new language and culture that expanded my young teenage mind. As I learned more and more I came to understand the courage, sacrifice, and downright balls it takes to leave your family, home, culture, and language and risk everything to come to America. Their willingness to rewrite their story and make up life as they went along was a quality we shared, and it bridged the chasm of language until I could speak fluent Spanish.

In the beginning I acted out phrases and naively tried to add an EL and an O to every word, like EL WATCH-O or EL HAT-O. Note to all aspiring Spanish speakers: the Spanish translation of embarrassed is not "embarazado," which I learned the hard way when I inadvertently told a group of people that I was pregnant!

One of my favorite ways to learn was to translate music. I would buy bootleg Spanish cassettes at the flea market for a dollar. Then, with pen in hand, I would listen and translate the songs with a Spanish/English dictionary. My favorite music was by a band called Los Bukis, fronted by a passionate singer and brilliant songwriter named Marco Antonio Solís (El Buki) who has an eerie resemblance to the pirate in the Captain Morgan Rum commercials. If you haven't seen those, picture a Mexican Jesus Christ in a silk shirt unbuttoned to the navel.

His lyrics were mesmerizing and so complex that sometimes I couldn't find the words in a standard dictionary. That was the case with the word "libidinoso," so I set out asking everyone at the flea market what it meant. No one could explain it. Finally, I found the definition in one of those really thick resource dictionaries. It meant lustful, as in the characteristic of someone who would say anything to be with you, and then leave you.

Years later, Marco would become a friend and a client and we would laugh at the thought of my broken Spanish as I tried to pronounce such a complex word. And how funny it was that I had learned to say "lust" in Spanish before I knew how to say spoon or fork.

As my Spanish progressed I became an ambassador between the Spanish-speaking vendors and the man who owned the flea market, Glen. Glen had a big heart, and once the language barrier was broken we solved many vendor issues together—simple things that showed the Hispanic seller base we cared, like printing our policies in both English and Spanish and making bilingual public address announcements. We also began hiring local Spanish bands to perform on the beer patio, a plan that increased shopping traffic and foreshadowed my future career as a concert promoter.

Glen was a scrappy entrepreneur who built the flea market from a small indoor operation in East San Jose to the huge outdoor parking lot of a six-theater drive-in complex. He was tall with grey hair, and had the air of a man who loved a challenge and who rarely failed to win. I had never met a millionaire before. His humility and accessibility opened my eyes to the impossible thought that I, too, could be a millionaire someday. After all, this guy was no different from me.

Glen had a hobby of panning for gold in the mountains of northern California. He often would bring vials of gold dust to the flea market and tell stories of his lone prospecting on the Feather River. Soon his hobby became more serious and he began looking at real mining opportunities in South America. Before I knew it he was planning a trip to Bolivia, and as the resident Spanish/English speaker I was asked to go along as a translator. My Spanish was nowhere good enough, but to me that didn't matter. The world was expanding like a trip through Willy Wonka's Chocolate Factory and I was going joyfully along for the ride.

This was my first trip to … well … anywhere … so I quickly figured out how to get a passport and the necessary vaccinations. I also had to talk to my high school teachers as finals were coming and I would miss them. Initially I assumed they would share my enthusiasm, but that idea quickly burst as teacher after teacher told me I was crazy and could not miss the tests. My "you-can't-tell-me-what-to-do" blood boiled, and as politely as an 18-year-old boy can (which is never all that polite), I told them I was going and that was that. And so it was.

Bolivia was the Wild West, an untamed land high in the Andes. We arrived in La Paz, a city I would learn had two faces. The public face had a flea market environment with vendors and beggars on every corner. It was poor—dirt poor—and the seemingly endless sea of begging children was heartbreaking. The second face of La Paz, behind the scenes, was where the wealth and power lived, behind gated walls with manicured lawns, chauffeurs, and maids.

I smile now at the precocious young man faking his way, translating meetings with government officials and businessmen. They must have thought we were crazy. We went from meeting to meeting exploring gold mining opportunities. Nothing could stop us. That is, except altitude sickness, which hit some of our group hard. I remember one especially traumatic moment when I walked into my friend's hotel room only to find him sitting on the toilet with his face in the sink, unsure which end would explode first!

Returning from Bolivia, I quickly began to gain more responsibility at the flea market. I moved from the parking lots, to a supervisor, to VP of Operations and up and up—all the while improving my Spanish. I immersed myself in the Mexican culture: music, TV, sports.

The biggest icon of the time was the boxing champion Julio César Chávez. He was more than a boxer, he was a national hero to the immigrants I knew, a Mexican Muhammad Ali who conquered the sport of boxing while speaking Spanish and proudly carrying the Mexican flag.

One weekend while I was working at the flea market, a friend called to invite me to Las Vegas. I was only 20 at the time, too young to be in the casinos, but the thought of seeing Sin City was too much to pass up. So I bought a $49 round-trip ticket on Southwest Airlines and headed to Vegas.

When I arrived I met up with my friends and we were surprised to see that Julio César Chávez would be fighting the following weekend. I didn't have the money to buy a ticket and had to work at the flea market over the weekend, so I opted instead to attend Julio's free public workout the following day.

Chávez is a small man (like the size of your teenage son) with brown hair and brown eyes and chiseled features. But that isn't what I noticed about him. What jumped out at me was his aura. There was an energy about him, an intensity I had never seen before. Like a superhero with a force field around him.

I stood there captivated until I noticed a man standing close by wearing a "Team Chávez" tracksuit. I asked him if he worked for Chávez. He smiled, apparently impressed that I could speak Spanish, and told me he was the fighter's brother, Rodolfo. We hit it off immediately and after an hour of conversation I was taking a picture with Julio.

In parting, Rodolfo said nonchalantly, "You should come to the next fight in two months in San Antonio." I'm sure he said it off the cuff, like what rock bands say to every fan they meet, but to me it was real. I decided then and there that nothing would stop me from being at that fight.

When I returned to the flea market, no one believed my story. They laughed and patted me on the back like I was a toddler saying he could fly. But I was undeterred. I sold the ice cream truck and bought a plane ticket to San Antonio and a thousand dollar ringside ticket to the fight. I did some investigating and found the hotel where Chávez would be staying and then booked a room for myself at San Antonio's finest hotel, with some financial support from my boss Glen.

The days ticked off the calendar so slowly, like all the analogies of paint drying and watched pots boiling rolled into one. When the date of my flight finally came I said goodbye to my friends at the flea market. Every time I was asked when I would be returning, I gave the same answer: "On Monday unless Chávez invites me back to Mexico with him." This would elicit the familiar laugh, and a "Jason's crazy" response. I didn't care.

I had decided that I could be a translator for Chávez and, with the help of my trusty bilingual dictionary, wrote a letter of explanation that I planned to give to his brother when I arrived in San Antonio, once again wildly overestimating my Spanish fluency. Then off I went to San Antonio, armed with my ringside ticket, translator letter, and my passport in case the invitation to Mexico came.

When I arrived at my hotel I located Rodolfo. I proudly gave him the letter, which I believed outlined my desire to be a translator. He stared at me blankly for a long time before asking if I wanted to be a mechanic.

"A mechanic? No, why?" I said.

His smile was sarcastic as he pointed to the letter. There it was: instead of "translator" I had written "transmission," like automatic or stick shift! Needless to say, that was the end of my translator aspirations and the beginning of a longstanding joke about Jason the grease monkey.

I spent an amazing week tagging along to press conferences, dinners, and weigh-ins. When fight time came I offered to trade my ticket to Rodolfo in exchange for credentials so I could stay with them instead of sitting down in the crowd.

If you ever see a video of the locker room before the fight, I'm the tall white guy surrounded by Chávez's Mexican team, all of us wearing the traditional red headband with Chávez's name on it. My head stuck out a foot above everyone else's, with an "I can't believe I'm here!" grin pasted to my face. I looked out of place but didn't even notice, I was living the dream.

I enjoyed the after-fight party with Rodolfo and the Chávez team. As night turned to morning, Rodolfo looked at me and said, "Do you want to come to Mexico with us? We have a large plane and you can fly with us." It was all I could do to contain myself. I couldn't believe it. My prediction to my friends at the flea market was about to come true.

So I was off to Mexico with one of the biggest boxing stars on the planet. I thought I had truly made it. This was the start of a longtime friendship and the next step in my young life, one that would start a series of wilder and wilder adventures. What also came with this step was one of the most important realizations of all ...

... I had the power to make things happen, to make even the most far-off dreams come true. All I had to do was believe.

· 5 ·

MY LITTLE GIRL

I ALWAYS KNEW I WOULD BE A DAD. MAYBE IT WAS ALL THOSE YEARS spent with my mom at the day-care centers where she worked. Or maybe it was a deep-down desire to be the man my father never was. In any case, I just knew.

Glen's son and I had started a side business at the flea market selling advertising on the back of the parking receipts. We got the idea while buying a pack of gum at the grocery store. After paying, we got the receipt and the cashier pointed out some money-saving coupons on the back. The moment we saw that we knew what we had to do.

After a brief conversation with Glen, during which we promised to pay the $500 per month printing fee for the parking receipts, I was in the advertising business.

Down the street from the flea market was a taco shop called Taquería Garcia. I met the owner, José, and I convinced him to buy some ads. We ended up becoming friends. He was a jolly man, always laughing and smiling and telling jokes. I would visit him for lunch on a regular basis and that's where I met my first wife, Claudia.

I'm not going to talk much about Claudia because this isn't that kind of book—the kind where I tell you all the reasons why I was too young to get married or how Claudia wasn't the one for me. What I will tell you is that when I met Claudia she had a daughter named Nataly who stole my heart. Nataly's father had left, which left a void in her life ... a void I was all too familiar with from my own childhood.

The first time I met Nataly was at the *taquería*. She was a precious little girl, short, with a round face and chubby red cheeks pressed up against the edge of her glasses. She waddled around the taco shop like a curly-haired penguin. I reached out to hold her hand and say hi and she fell down. She was a year-and-a-half old at the time and this was a catastrophe. Sitting on the floor, looking at me like I was the bogeyman, she wailed. You know the kind of wail ... the one that causes everyone to look at you like you're an abusive S.O.B. who made a little kid cry. She wailed and I sat there red in the face.

As with most fathers and daughters this wouldn't be the last time I would carelessly make her cry. Like on her second birthday when I hired a Barney impersonator to come to her party. She took one look at that big, purple monster and ran. She hid under her bed for the entire party while the other kids played.

But all the tough moments would be blanketed by the warm love of a father and daughter who chose each other. Since I only worked three days a week at the flea market, I would pick her up from the babysitter while her mom was working. We would walk, holding hands, at the Happy Hollow Zoo. We would talk to each other in animal voices; laugh and play hide-and-seek. Then we'd go to Baskin-Robbins and eat ice cream and talk about all we had seen.

When Nataly was around six I adopted her. She was so proud to say that she had chosen me, and when the judge was finalizing the proceeding, she stopped him. You see, he had assumed the round-faced little girl in pink glasses had nothing to say ... he was wrong. This was her life and her adoption and she wanted to tell all who would listen that she was choosing me as her daddy.

The next year Nataly made another declaration. She now had a brother, Kevin. She notified our friends and family with a heartfelt, hand-drawn birth announcement: "My baby brother." Nataly was shy and quiet about some things, but when it came to manifesting the family she wanted, she was the boss.

By 1999 Claudia and I divorced and I was awarded custody of the children. Since the legal fees had cost me my house and what little savings I had, the kids and I moved into a two-bedroom apartment in a small complex.

Our day went something like this. We would wake up at 6:00 a.m., eat breakfast and get ready for work and school. Then Nataly, Kevin, and I would drive first to Nataly's school and drop her off. Then Kevin and I would drive to the day-care center my mom ran where Kevin would spend the day. I would arrive at my office, which was down the street, by 8:30 or 9:00. I'd work until 2:00 p.m. and then I would drive back across town to pick up Nataly from school and take her to my mom's day-care center. Then back to work until 6:00 p.m., after which I would hustle back to the day-care center to pick up the kids before closing. Add to this I was running my own business as a concert promoter.

The schedule was as exhausting as it sounds. Not to mention that I couldn't help noticing the irony—or perhaps destiny is a better word—that I was reliving my mom's single parent life.

It was also beautiful as the kids and I were spending so much time together. My travel and work had to be planned around them. We bonded like never before. Through the stress and the chaos of divorce and the life of single parenthood came a lifetime bond that bears its fruits today in the unique relationship we share.

There is a version of this story in which I, the dad on the white horse, rode into Nataly's life and rescued her ... became her father ... spent my young adult years providing her a life of love and opportunity ... put her through school ... loved and supported her. All that is true.

There is also another version in which an amazing little girl from a broken family manifested the life she had always dreamed of ... and in the process rescued me. That little girl with the beaming smile and curly hair became the one constant in my life, giving me a love that was always there ... the only love that never left me. Her powerful ability to create the life she wanted would benefit our family.

After my second divorce, it was Nataly who convinced me to buy a dog for the kids. Then in the midst of her teenage years, walking the tightrope between hating and loving me, she put teenage angst aside and helped her little brother build a PowerPoint presentation, as she had seen me do so many times for my boss. Slide after slide, they laid out the reasons a dog would be good for our family: love ... comfort ... companionship ... even hypo-allergenic. It had both their names on it, but I knew it was all Nataly. And she was right.

It would be Nataly years later who led our family toward the healthy habits we now follow. She would pester us, harass us to watch documentaries like *Fat, Sick and Nearly Dead*; *Forks Over Knives*; *A Beautiful Truth*; and so many others. It took us years to listen, but once again Nataly led the way.

When I would finally find my soul mate and life partner, Christy, Nataly—then 20 years old—would play an almost seer-like role. Sharing with me later that when the three of us met innocently for the first time, she had gone home to tell her brother, "Today I met Daddy's wife." Something only a daughter could have known.

In the end, the truth is that Nataly and I chose each other. A man determined to be the kind of loving father he never had, and a little girl, a powerful creator, who wouldn't stop until she had formed her life like a story from her childhood fairy tale books.

Once upon a time they met in a taco shop, and through the everyday routine of life learned a lesson in family and love. A truth more important than blood or race or circumstance. Love … especially that of a daddy and his little girl … love is all that truly matters.

·6·

TEACHERS, COPS, AND FEDERAL COURT

WITHOUT A FATHER I WAS NOT ONLY IN NEED OF MENTORSHIP, I WAS also free to seek it out without feeling guilty about a jealous dad. So that's what I did. My life was blessed with an endless stream of father figures, big brothers, and teachers.

My sophomore year in high school I joined the JV football team. I wasn't a very good football player. The truth is I sucked, but being on the team made me part of "that crowd" so I suffered through the embarrassment of sitting on the bench in exchange for the perks of wearing the jersey around school.

At the start of the second semester I got my new class schedule and showed it to my friends.

"Oh no," they said. "You've got Mr. Allen. He hates football players and is the toughest teacher in the school. You've got to get out of that class."

So off I went to talk to Mr. Allen about transferring out of his class. When I arrived he greeted me with a stern, "What do you want?" He peered at me from behind reading glasses perched on the end of his nose and looked like a modern-day Archie Bunker. I glanced down at the football jersey I was wearing and thought, "Shit, bad choice of wardrobe."

I gave him some song and dance about why I wanted out of his class. I can't remember my reason although I'm sure I thought it was clever enough to deal with some old English teacher. But I had not met clever like Mr. Allen. No, even with all my street smarts and guts, I was no match for my soon-to-be mentor.

"Well kiddo," he said. "If you're the type of young man who quits before he starts or doesn't have the guts for a challenge that will improve his life, then sure, you can go find some other teacher who will hold your hand and baby you … ."

Baby me? Quit? No guts? Did he know who he was talking to?? I'm Jason Garner, I said to myself. I've never quit anything … I don't need to be babied! Why, I'll show you who you're dealing with!

That's what I thought. What managed to escape from my astonished lips was something more like, "Uh, no, ok, well, um, no, no, this is a misunderstanding. I'll be in class on Monday."

Of course this was exactly his plan. I had been played like a fiddle, and in the end it was for the best. Mr. Allen—Bruce—became my lifelong friend. He was my first mentor. He pushed me to my limits. The truth is he tortured me, always knowing exactly when to call on me to provide the maximum embarrassment.

"Let's see what our football star has to say … I'm sure Mr. Garner did the homework and has the answer for us … girls, Jason is looking for a date to the prom ... if you're interested he's the guy in the football jersey who didn't do his homework."

Rough, eh? Truth is he knew just how to motivate me.

He also lent me money to fix my broken-down Trans Am, gave me a dress shirt and tie to wear to my first school prom, and later served as a groomsman in my second marriage.

His favorite story was the summer I worked for him painting houses. He says I was a horrible employee. I had fallen in love for the first time with a girl named Michelle and showed up late for work nearly every day after spending the night at Michelle's house. I was tired and careless. My mind was lost in summer love and disinterested in mundane tasks like scraping and painting. I will never forget his face, tomato red, steam nearly venting from his ears, when I spilled a five-gallon can of paint on the roof of a house we were working on. It took me all day to clean it up. In the end, it was just one of many lessons Bruce taught me: "Look where you're going, Garner."

Mr. Allen was my first mentor, but not my last.

Phil, a San Jose police officer, was the head of security at the flea market. We became good friends, and he quickly took me under his wing. He was the father of two daughters, and I became the son he never had. If you remember the story about Bolivia and my friend wedged between the toilet and the sink, that was Phil. He taught me to change the oil in my car, or better stated, taught me to watch *him* change the oil in my car. I was never much of a dirty-hands kind of guy, as he noted when he refused to take me bear hunting, saying, "I'm not gonna take you up there and have to carry your bear down the mountain." I breathe a sigh of relief every time I remember that story, as I don't think I could forgive myself today, as a vegetarian, had I shot a bear.

Dan, another mentor of young Jason, was the lawyer for the flea market. I met him after a police officer filed a false police report against me. The problem started when our landlord, the drive-in movie company, decided to turn the drive-in into a huge indoor theater. It was a great idea for them but a violation of the flea market's lease that would severely damage our business. So we sued them and a nasty battle broke out. In addition to the legal dispute, we had a constant flow of problems as the flea market operated in the midst of dust and construction from the new project. Both the movie company and the flea market hired off-duty police officers to keep the peace, like a mini Cold War stand-off.

One day while walking around the flea market I noticed that Bob, a police officer who worked for the movie company, was walking out with a big box of fruits and vegetables. I assumed he had gotten it for free and decided to rib him.

"Hey Bob, wonder what your bosses at the police department would say about your taking free produce while in uniform?" I chuckled at my cleverness.

Well Officer Bob had a surprise for me. The next day he arrived at the flea market in his patrol car. On the way out he drove by me and said, "Watch your back, smart ass." I quickly found out what this meant when Phil informed me that Bob was claiming I had interfered with his attempt to arrest a suspect. His exact allegation was that I grabbed his arm while he was making an arrest and yelled, "Let him go, punk!" It was absurd, but I was scared nonetheless.

Officer Bob was a scary guy with a reputation for, well, creative police work. And now there was a police report and an open investigation against me.

Luckily the district attorney decided not to file charges and the complaint against me was dropped. But for me that wasn't enough. This was wrong and the self-righteous young man inside me needed justice.

I first tried to resolve the issue with the Internal Affairs Division at the police department. That got me nowhere. So I asked Glen if I could talk to his lawyer Dan, who at that time was representing the flea market in their litigation against the movie company. Glen agreed and offered to lend me the legal fees if necessary. I drove to Dan's office near the airport for a meeting and to tell him my story.

Dan is a kind man. He has warm energy that exudes from him like a welcome-home hug. He's the type of guy who is comfortable anywhere, from a board meeting to a coffee shop, and he makes friends everywhere he goes.

When he agreed to take my case I was shocked, although he did have one condition: I had to take a lie detector test. I was telling the truth so I agreed, even though the request took me aback. I had seen lie detector tests on TV, on shows like *Hawaii Five-0* and *Miami Vice*. They always looked a bit scary with wires and machines and lots of invasive questions. But if this is what it took, I would do it. I was hell-bent on getting my justice!

Dan and I drove to the same lie detector company the police department used. I was hooked up to the machines and the operator explained the procedure to me. "Be calm," he said. "Breathe normally." Be calm? Breathe normally? Was he nuts? I was ready to shit my pants!

Of course I passed the test. The only eventful moment came when he asked me if I had ever stolen from my employer. Knowing my boss would see the results, I swallowed deeply and admitted to taking five dollars from petty cash once in awhile to pay for a delivery pancake breakfast. I prayed Glen wouldn't see it, or at least would forgive me if he did.

Armed with my lie detector test results and a lawyer, I figured it was only a matter of time before Officer Bob would be begging for forgiveness. Of course the justice system isn't that simple. I was about to get a real-life civics class.

It turns out that suing a police officer isn't that easy. They are protected by a shield of immunity that allows them to do their job without a storm of legal suits. We had exhausted all the options until finally one late night at Dan's office we decided to start from scratch.

"Why did Bob file the report against you?" Dan asked.

"Because he's a shit for brains," I said, only half kidding.

"No really, why?" Dan pressed on: "What did he want to gain?"

"He wanted to scare me. But that didn't work."

"Exactly," Dan said. "He wanted to scare you so you wouldn't speak out against the movie company. And that, Jason, is a violation of your First Amendment rights!"

With that brilliant piece of legal strategy Dan and I were off to United States Federal Court. On the day of the hearing I arrived early in a suit and tie I'd purchased for $99 at Burlington Coat Factory. This was amazing. Here I was in federal court, fighting a crooked cop and defending my rights.

The judge was a short, Hispanic man who I believe was named Judge Escalante. He called Officer Bob into his chambers first and heard his side of the story. Then he called me in. His chambers looked like a scene from *Perry Mason*. Wood-paneled walls, a large desk, and a U.S. Federal Judge. To give you an idea, this was the same man who heard cases between the United States and foreign countries.

I told him my side of the story from beginning to end. He smiled warmly at me and said simply, "Young man, I believe you. What would you like me to do?"

I sat there astonished, unable to believe that a kid like me, with no money, no power, and no special connections was about to be vindicated against a man who wore a uniform, a badge, and a gun.

I thanked Judge Escalante and told him that I was requesting the police report be thrown out, that Officer Bob write me an apology, that I be granted a restraining order against further harassment by Officer Bob, and ... should I do it? I wondered. Why not?!

"Oh, and that I be paid ten thousand dollars for all the fear and anxiety. And while we're at it, pay my legal fees too." I held my breath, waiting for the judge to say, "Who do you think you are, kid?!"

Instead he calmly asked me to go back to the courtroom and said he would talk to the city attorney. Within a few minutes Judge Escalante entered the courtroom. He told Officer Bob to stand up. He admonished him for his actions. He read his decision, and it was exactly what I asked for. Then he told Officer Bob to look me in the eye and say he was sorry. Which he did. It was amazing, though, honestly, I could only think about the fact that I was about to have ten thousand dollars. Officer Bob at this point was an afterthought and would go from being a scary nemesis to a great story.

Dan, on the other hand, would become my brother and coach. He sold me my first cell phone, he hired me to help out in his law firm, he counseled me on life and love. To this day we share a special bond, enjoying our journey through life and remembering the days when we fought the law and won!

There were so many great mentors in my young life. Men who filled the role of father and gave me the guidance I needed to grow. Starting with Bruce in high school and continuing to this very day, what began as sadness in my life—not having a dad—turned into a beautiful lesson said best through the words of grumpy old Mr. Allen: "Kiddo, you are one lucky young man."

·7·

BECOMING A CONCERT PROMOTER

SITTING IN THE ELEGANT RESTAURANT OF THE FAIRMONT HOTEL IN SAN Jose, I felt out of place. Rodolfo Chávez, Julio's brother, and I had just completed a large sponsorship deal for Julio with a company in San Jose. After we signed the deal, Ruben, the head of the company's ad agency and the man who brokered the deal, suggested I take them out to dinner to celebrate. He knew just the place, he said. That's how we ended up in the nicest restaurant in town.

When the menu came I noticed there were no prices. I thought that was strange. No prices? I'd heard about these kinds of places, restaurants where money was no object, so why bother to list the price?

The first time I went to Mexico with Rodolfo and Julio they joked, telling me, "Don't worry about money, Jason ... ." Then, just as I had dreams of a lavish trip and luxurious gifts, they added, "Because we don't have any!"

I laughed then because they DID have money. But I wasn't laughing that night in San Jose, staring at the priceless menu. I didn't have the kind of money it took to be there. In fact, all I had in my pocket was a check for ten grand, my share of the sponsorship deal; and a secured credit card with a $500 limit, of which I had already used $250. Uh oh. The remaining $250 wasn't going to cut it in a restaurant like this.

I ordered what I assumed would be the cheapest menu item, a garden salad. You know the trick. "I'm not that hungry, bring me a salad please. Just a normal green salad."

Then I excused myself and went to the pay phone (this was before cell phones). I dialed the number on the back of my secured credit card. After a few minutes on hold an operator answered. I told her I wanted to transfer $250 from my checking account onto my credit card, giving me $500 of credit on the card. And maybe, just maybe, I would squeak by the night without being embarrassed. Only problem, their computers were down. "I'm really sorry, sir, but there is nothing I can do," the attendant told me.

Oh shit.

I went back to the table and sat down. "Shall we order wine?" Ruben, who looked like a classy Geraldo Rivera, asked. You have to be fucking kidding me, I thought. First you suggest I invite everyone out and now you want to order wine!?

"None for me," I said, trying to hide the fact that I wanted to hit this guy. Of course everyone else wanted wine, so we ended up ordering not one, but two bottles.

When the bill came, my fears were validated. It was $450. I must have turned white … or red … or maybe green. Hell, I don't know, but whatever it was, when Ruben looked at me, he winked and said, "I got it."

PHEW!

That's how I became a concert promoter.

What?

Ha ha. Just wanted to make sure you were paying attention. Actually it IS how I went from working at the flea market to promoting concerts, but there's a little more story to fill in.

After nearly causing me the most embarrassing night of my life and then rescuing me from the same near miss, Ruben and I became friends. I was managing the flea market by this time and he was running the ad agency and promoting Spanish-language concerts. We would get together from time to time to have dinner or a drink.

One day Ruben called me. He had a problem and thought I could help. He and some partners were promoting a Spanish-language dance concert at the San Jose Convention Center. They had a ton of money invested and needed a big turnout.

Good for you, I thought. But what does this have to do with me?

It turned out that the same night of their dance, Mike Tyson was fighting in Las Vegas, a fight that would be shown on TV via Pay-per-view. It was Tyson's first fight since being released from jail and was sure to be a huge contest that would have everyone glued to their TV sets.

Wow, bad luck. But I still didn't see the connection to me.

"You know all the boxing people," Ruben said. "So I want you to figure out how to show the fight at my concert so people won't stay home and ruin my event."

Okay. Got it. The truth was, though, that I knew Chávez and that was it. I didn't know how to buy the rights to televise a fight at a dance concert. I didn't even know where to start.

But what did I say? "No problem. Leave it to me. I'll work it out." This sounded like a big money-making opportunity and I wasn't going to let a small detail like not having any idea what I was doing stand in my way!

Remember there was no Google in those days, no Internet, no easy way to figure out something unknown and new. I started making phone calls. I called Rodolfo, who told me to call so-and-so. Then that person connected me with someone else. And on and on until I finally ended up on the phone with the right person who controlled the rights I was looking for.

The first thing I learned is that what I was looking to do was called "closed circuit," and that it would require a satellite, projectors, some big screens, and a substantial payment to the agent I had on the phone.

Okay, at least now I knew what I was talking about. I called Ruben and told him I had it all figured out and it would cost ... well, I told him it would cost double what the agent told me. I had to make some money too, right?

After a bit of negotiation with Ruben, then the agent, then Ruben again, then the agent again, then Ruben for the last time and finally the agent to close the deal, I was now officially in the closed-circuit boxing business!

Oh, and once the day of the event came around and I delivered on my deal with Ruben, I was also $20,000 richer!

In 1996 the owners of the flea market sold the business. As the manager I received a bonus of $100,000. I had mixed emotions as my job was ending, I would be moving on from the place where I had learned so much (my makeshift business school), but I was also excited because I had received the most money I had seen up to that point. I took a little time off to enjoy my new-found wealth.

Then one day my old friend Ruben called. He'd left the ad agency and had dedicated himself full time to the concert business. He had just secured a new venue for Mexican concerts and rodeos and asked me to help him run the venue and its concessions, like I had learned at the flea market. Concerts? Rodeos? Well I'd never done that before, but okay, I thought, I have nothing else going on.

I began working with Ruben. He had two or three events a month. Ruben was booking the bands and selling the tickets. I was overseeing security, ushers, and the concession stands. It was a perfect match. We got along great. The business performed well. Soon Ruben suggested we become partners.

We opened Alvarez and Garner, LLC and, after selling gum and dictionaries, filling my ice cream truck with cleats and roses and anything else I could find, running a flea market, selling advertising on the back of parking receipts, working as a legal assistant, winning a lawsuit in federal court, hanging out with the biggest boxer in the world, selling a closed-circuit boxing match, and attending a fateful dinner that was nearly a disaster, I was now a concert promoter.

Ruben and I struggled to get our business going until we had a stroke of luck. With the help of our friend Hector, who knew a powerful agent in Hollywood, we landed the highly anticipated California concerts for the new star, Enrique Iglesias. Enrique was one of the first big pop stars in the Spanish-language concert market. These were his first shows, and he was playing big basketball and hockey arenas. Landing Enrique was a big deal for our little company, and something that put us on the map.

I remember being so nervous about the big investment that I called every record store in the area to check on his sales, which were huge of course. Having called to be sure helped me sleep better.

We promoted shows in San Diego, San Jose, and Sacramento on that tour. They were all big successes and the shows caught the eye of the legendary concert company, Bill Graham Presents. Up until that point Spanish-language music was under the radar of the big boys, but Enrique changed all that. He was a huge star, with big-time management and agents and a name that everyone recognized from the success of his dad, Julio Iglesias.

Suddenly, Ruben and I weren't the small-time guys promoting

Mexican rodeos, we were the answer to the question, "Who did those shows with Enrique Iglesias?"

At the behest of Enrique's manager Juan Carlos and his agents Peter and Jorge, we met with the owners of Bill Graham Presents at their office in San Francisco. Bill Graham, the founder, was a legend in the concert business. In fact, more than a legend, he was one of the founders of the scene. From his Fillmore Ballrooms in San Francisco and New York he helped establish Janis Joplin, the Grateful Dead, Jefferson Starship, and many, many others, which he parlayed into one of the most successful concert companies in the business. After his death his key employees purchased the business and continued the successful tradition he started.

So there we were, Ruben and I, sitting in the lobby of BGP, as it was called for short. The walls were lined with posters of bands that I, as a poor kid, had dreamed of seeing but had never had the money or connections to see. U2, Madonna, Metallica, and legends like The Rolling Stones, Jimi Hendrix, and The Doors. This was the big league and truthfully, I was scared.

Finally we were ushered back to meet with Gregg and Sherry, two of the owners and principal operators of the company. We had a pleasant conversation about which I don't remember much. After telling our stories and talking about the rise of the Hispanic concert business, Gregg got down to business. "So here's the deal, guys. This Spanish-language concert stuff is heating up. Acts like Enrique Iglesias are making real money and filling big arenas. This is a business we want to be in. We're the best at putting on the show, but we don't know how to market to Spanish speakers. You do. So let's work together."

Sounded simple enough. But Ruben and I had heard stories about the big-time concert business. This was a cutthroat industry. We didn't want to end up being chewed up and spit out.

Ruben spoke up. "Well Gregg, that sounds interesting, what do you have in mind?"

"I assume you guys don't have the money to play at this level," Gregg said. "So we'll fund the shows, do all the production. You guys do the marketing and we'll pay you a fee for the work."

This was exactly what we'd been worried about. If we went to work for these guys, making a fee, we would lose our identity and never grow our company the way we wanted. The only way this would work would be a true partnership. Gregg was right: we didn't have the money to play at this level. But we did have balls, so we bluffed.

Once again Ruben spoke: "We want to be partners, 50/50," he said.

"Hmm," Gregg said. "I only have one question for you. If one of our shows loses $200,000 do you have the money to write a check for 50% … $100,000?"

"Gregg, do you really think we'd be here if we didn't?" Ruben said, and that's how we became partners with Bill Graham Presents. Ruben's poker face disguised the truth that we had few bucks and big dreams.

Our first concert together was a sold-out show with Luis Miguel at the San Jose Arena. The show began as Gregg, Sherry, Ruben, and I all stood together at the back of the arena floor. Gregg turned to Ruben and me and said, "Great job, partners." Ruben and I smiled confidently, then sighed very private sighs of relief that the show had made money and our cover hadn't been blown.

From there our fortunes turned and we became the top Spanish-language promoters in the area. Our partnership with BGP on the big shows gave us prestige and the ability to do more because of their big infrastructure. Everything was going great.

Then it wasn't. Ruben and I had opened a new rodeo arena at the fairgrounds in San Jose called Plaza San Jose. It had 6,000 seats and was a great new venue with high hopes that, unfortunately, didn't pan out.

We had put all of our money into the venue, expecting it would be an immediate hit. It wasn't and we were hemorrhaging money. Show after show too few fans turned out, and we suffered loss after loss. It was a new venue, and new venues take time to establish, something we didn't know at the time.

One night sitting in the office we reviewed the books. It was worse than we thought. We were $250,000 in the hole, we didn't have enough money to pay our bills, and our creditors were starting to catch on. We had two options: close the company or figure this out. We agreed to sleep on it and make our decision the next day.

I went home and looked at my daughter, Nataly, and my little baby boy, Kevin. What was I going to do? I had never failed before. I had scraped through tough times when I was all alone, but now I had a family to look out for. Fuck, what had I gotten myself into? My stomach was in knots. All night I tossed and turned with my mind racing. I was desperately searching for an answer. At some point I must have fallen asleep because the morning sun woke me up. I was still on the couch where I'd sat the night before, agonizing.

I got dressed and went to the office. Ruben was already there. I looked him in the eyes.

"We can't fail Ruben," I said. "We won't. We have too much riding on this. I know we can turn this around. Let's stick it out and dig our way out of this mess."

I waited for Ruben's reply, searching his face for an inkling of what he was thinking. A tear fell from his eye. Then he said, "*Vámonos* partner, let's do it."

We had decided to be honest with our creditors. Ruben and I divided up the list and, one by one, we called them and admitted the truth of our situation. We agreed to call those to whom we were closest. This was the only time I remember not wanting to be the one with the best contacts.

"We're asking for your help. If you help keep us afloat, we'll set up a payment plan and pay you back every penny. If you say no, we will have to close and go bankrupt and you'll get nothing."

It was a gut-wrenching day. We went from being the big dogs in town to well ... dirty old stray dogs that no one wanted around. By the end of the day, we learned what balls really were. We had the courage to look our problem in the face. Most importantly, every single creditor agreed to our terms.

Alvarez and Garner was still in business. Now we needed a plan.

It was simple. We went back to basics and booked only sure deals, shows that had performed well in the past or really big-name artists. We also diversified, just as BGP had done with us. We looked for smaller niche promoters and partnered with them on shows we hadn't done before—salsa dances, comedy shows, anything we saw that would make us money with minimum risk.

It took us a year to pay everyone back. We scrimped by, living on less, watching every dollar, wasting nothing—no more sushi dinners, no more trips, and no more expensive bottles of tequila after a successful show. The big shots had learned a big-time lesson in humility and responsibility. And we succeeded, a success far greater than any concert.

Years later, a radio station president (one of those I spoke with that embarrassing day asking for leniency on our debt) was doing business with an employee of mine at Live Nation. When the employee asked him how he knew me, he told the employee our story. Then he said, "What they did took a lot of courage and honesty, and that's why I trust Jason today."

Who would have guessed that my integrity would be judged from what, at the time, was one of the worst moments of my life?

Another important lesson learned: the importance of facing life head-on, humbly accepting the moment as it is, and being true to my values.

·8·

NATIONAL TRAGEDY, AND A ROCK 'N' ROLL BUS RIDE

I WAS BUSILY TRYING TO GET NATALY AND KEVIN READY FOR SCHOOL and myself ready for the office when the phone rang. It was too early for a call, one of those weird moments when you know there isn't good news ringing through the line.

So I answered. It was my friend Chela, the manager of the Mexican rock band El Tri and wife of their flamboyant front man, Alex. Ruben and I had met them a few years earlier at a concert we organized for the band. From there our relationship blossomed and we put on a few more shows together. Chela took a liking to me and recognized my ability to make money for them in the States, so she gave us the opportunity to promote their entire U.S. tour that year. But this call wasn't about business. She was crying.

"Chela, what's wrong?" I asked.

"Aren't you watching?" she said, incredulous, not believing that I wasn't as upset as she was.

"Watching what, Chela? I'm getting the kids ready for school."

"Your country is under attack!" she screamed.

I laughed. "Chela that's ridiculous. Who told you that?"

"Turn on your TV, Jason!"

So I did. And I saw ... the un-seeable.

That's how I found out about the terrorist attacks of September 11th.

It's also how I ended up on a bus later that month, zipping through the middle of the country with Alex, Chela, and El Tri.

After the attacks, traveling by plane with anyone, let alone with a ragtag group of rock stars, was really difficult. Still in shock from what was taking place in my country, I spent the week following that phone call canceling the flights I had booked for our tour and contracting a bus instead.

It won't be that bad, I thought. We would see the country from the road. A rock band and I, just like in the movies. There will be singing, strumming, drinking, laughing, and storytelling. Just like Willie Nelson's song "On the Road Again," only in real life.

So it was that one day in late September I met El Tri in Indianapolis to start our magical mystery tour. They were flying in from Mexico. I arrived earlier to make sure everything went smoothly. The moment I got into the airport I knew I had made the right decision to tour via bus. Security was tight, really tight, and there was an uneasy tension in the air. A "What's going to happen next?" kind of tension I had never experienced in America. It was frightening and sad.

The band played a show that night in Indianapolis. If you have never seen El Tri you should. Many Americans don't know them, but in their country they are rock royalty, The Rolling Stones of Mexico. Their music is straightforward classic rock, like Chuck Berry meets Lynyrd Skynyrd. And Alex ... well ... Alex is one of a kind. Leather jacket, sunglasses, Weird Al Yankovic hair, a laugh that just makes you smile, lyrics that define rock and roll, an Ozzy Osbourne persona of you never know what's he's going to say next, and a bass guitar shaped like a middle finger—a friendly fuck you to the world. To top it off? The tip of the middle finger of that bass guitar has been molded like the tip of ... how do I say this delicately? Get the picture yet? No? The guitar tip is shaped like the tip of a giant penis. During the shows when things get really hot he shoots milk out of the guitar from a hidden syringe. What did I tell you? A rock star ... *the* Mexican rock star.

Okay, let's get to the bus ride. After the show in Indianapolis we got on our beautiful touring bus. Everyone was happy and we set out to our next destination. We all started to drink. Then the scene I had envisioned happened. The band got their instruments out. Guitar. Harmonica. Bass guitar. And soon there was music and singing and ... it was ... yeah ... rock promoter heaven! One of those moments you always dream of as a kid. On tour with a rock band. Just like the movie *Almost Famous*.

In the midst of all this fun and excitement and my dreams coming true, I didn't really pay attention to the rules the bus driver had yelled back to us. I also must not have noticed the sign posted outside the bathroom door because I was about to commit a rock tour bus no-no. A big no-no.

But I didn't know that yet. Not until the toilet overflowed. Not until the smell started wafting through the bus. Not until the driver, furious, stopped the bus and made us all get off so he could clean up the mess ... my mess.

As we stood there on the side of the road, shivering in the cold, Alex turned to me and whispered a lesson that would serve me well for the rest of my concert career. "Jason, don't you know? You don't ever ... ever. I mean never ... ever ... shit on the bus!"

· 9 ·

MY FIRST GURU

BY 2003, I HAD REMARRIED AND MOVED FROM SAN JOSE, CALIFORNIA TO Beverly Hills. The work Ruben and I had done with Bill Graham Presents led to an offer by Clear Channel Entertainment to work in their Spanish-language concert division.

The job required I move to Los Angeles, and after looking all around for housing and schools for the kids, I settled on an apartment in Beverly Hills. The place was out of my price range, but since it allowed me to enroll my children in great schools I made it work.

I was transitioning from being a big fish in a little pond to a teeny-tiny fish in an ocean. I had gone from running shows in a small geographical area to being responsible for the entire U.S. While this was a big step up, one I had been dreaming of for a long time, I realized when I got to LA how far down the totem pole I really was.

I had become one of the most prominent Spanish-language concert promoters; Clear Channel, on the other hand, was huge. I was one of several thousand employees. As one of my early mentors in the company said to me: "This company is so big, and you'll have so much autonomy,

you'll be lonely despite being surrounded by people everywhere you turn."
He was right.

I tried to approach the job as a learning experience. I had never worked in a big company before. For the first time in years, I got a guaranteed paycheck (which was good) and I had a boss (which sometimes wasn't). The latter took some getting used to. A lot of getting used to, actually. The truth was while I knew I was growing, I wasn't happy. I didn't like my boss and was worried I would never get ahead. That all changed when I met Michael Rapino.

I'd been sent to meet him by my boss's boss's boss. Michael was the company's president of Europe. The continent. I say this not because you don't know that Europe is a continent, but because I had never thought that big before. I was content to be in charge of a niche of music, a language. But this man, not ten years older than I, was running an entire continent.

He smiled at me and held up a finger to say, "Gimme a minute to finish this call." So I looked around. The first thing I noticed was how normal his office was. It was the same size as mine. There was nothing fancy on the walls. No awards or self-congratulatory mementos, just a place to get the day's work done. The second thing I noticed was that there were clocks, several of them representing the various time zones he oversaw, another reminder of the expansive world in which he operated. The third was the level of intensity in his conversation. His voice was calm, cool, collected. But there was a passion, a purpose to his words, as if each of them had been specifically selected for its strategic value, like moves on a chess board.

When he finished his call he looked up and smiled at me like a man not sure of who was sitting in his office, or why. "What's up?" he said.

For the next hour we talked. Well, really, I talked for a few minutes about some business thing I was told to review with him. Then he talked about business, but more about life. It's a skill I would learn that Michael had mastered—taking a business talk and weaving in a personal connection, showing you he cared beyond the dollars and cents.

The next time I saw Michael was a couple of weeks later at a concert. The hugely popular Mexican rock band Maná was playing at the Universal Amphitheater. I was there to see the band and he had come to see his friend, the band's agent.

I ran into him in the hallway backstage and then we took a walk. He told me his story. Born in a small town in Canada, he had become a local beer rep for the Canadian beer maker Labatt Brewing Company. What a great job. He was basically the kid who brought all the beer to the parties and got paid for it. There he met his mentor, Hugo Powell, who, like Michael would later do for me, inspired him to new heights. With this new inspiration Michael climbed the corporate ladder.

Then one night, sitting in a diner in Toronto, he pondered his future. What did he want to do? Stay at Labatt's? Further ascend the ranks of leadership? No, he had always dreamed of being a concert promoter, of connecting artists and fans on huge stages. So he penciled out his dream on a napkin, one he would later show me.

"One day I will run a global concert company."

His life had been a series of adventures and lessons, like mine, and this inspired me. While I was trying to find my greatness and break out of the crowded pack at this big company, he had done it.

But what most impressed me that night, the thing I will always remember, the part of Michael that would make me love AND admire him, was that he cared. He asked me questions. He asked me about my dreams. Then he asked me how he could help.

I told him my story, how I had started booking bands at the flea market, then the Mexican rodeo, Enrique Iglesias, Alvarez and Garner, and now head of Clear Channel's Spanish-language division. I shared with him my fears, how I felt lost in a big company and that I knew I had much to offer. He listened and offered to help.

Little did I know how much he would help me, how that one conversation, that one connection, would change the course of my life.

A few days later I got a call from Arthur, the top promoter in the company, asking me to come see him. He asked me what I was working on, introduced me to his team, and offered their assistance. He smiled, told me he'd heard good things about me, that I was a star.

Then more calls, and more offers of help.

What was going on?

It turned out that Michael had sent out a note saying he had met a young star who was stuck in a dead-end division and who could use some mentorship. As he would say to me later, "Perhaps you've noticed your visibility has increased a bit since we spoke."

It was a lesson. A lesson in the value of raising your hand. Of being seen. Of having the courage to step outside your comfort zone to see what the world has to offer. It was also a lesson of how a leader gives back. He had been helped by his mentor, and now he was helping me—one of countless lessons I would learn from Michael.

Soon Michael was not just running the European division, but was CEO of the company. I was the trusted sidekick whose office was right next door. Project to project, job to job, my visibility rose. Michael would give me a project and I would do whatever it took to deliver. When I stumbled he would pick me up and then push me until I got it right. This would become our relationship.

What I lacked in formal education I made up for with street smarts, on-the-job learning, and reading. I would walk by Michael's office, see what he was reading, and then go buy a copy.

I wanted to be a leader, like Michael. So I had to learn. I read...and read ...and read. Anything I could get my hands on to learn the fundamentals of big business. I started with the biographies of great leaders and entrepreneurs. Carnegie. Welch. Iacocca. One day Michael recommended I read Peter Drucker, known as the father of modern business. I started with his classic *The Effective Executive* and read all 38 of his remaining books.

But my greatest lessons, the ones that impacted me beyond anything I'd learned anywhere else, came from the late-night classes disguised as "catch up" conversations in Michael's office. Michael would recount his day or lessons from his life and I would listen, taking mental notes and then applying what I learned to my job. He would needle me, poke and jab, provoking the leader in me to emerge.

One of my favorite lessons was a story about when Michael was still at Labatt's. The company was expanding into Latin America and Michael was charged with building the marketing campaign. He worked diligently, night and day, building the proposal that he was to present to his mentor and the board. When the day of the big meeting arrived, he strode in with his presentation. He went through the marketing spend, the advertising, the slogans, and all the brilliant ideas he had mustered up for this big presentation. At the end of his talk his mentor, Hugo, asked one simple question.

"What is the most important factor in beer distribution in Latin America?"

Michael replied quickly: "Cooler space. The whole game is won or lost by getting our beer in the coolers. Because the retail outlets are mom-and-pop, they have small coolers. That's why our advertising has to be spot on so that customers will demand our product and retailers will carry it in their small coolers."

"Hmm," his mentor said.

"Hmm" is a powerful expression. Perhaps the most powerful. It's an expression I've learned to use often, one that says everything while giving up nothing. It's an acknowledgement for what someone has told you, an absorption of their message, an understanding of the moment without judgment.

"Coolers?" Hugo said. "The whole game comes down to coolers?"

"Yes," Michael said.

"Well, why don't we buy them coolers? Spend all the money on coolers stocked with our beer."

This story would become a classic in our company. The story that Michael, and then I and others, would use to make a point when someone was complicating a simple issue. "What are the coolers in this situation?" we would ask our team.

Michael's lessons weren't limited to business. He became a life coach for me. His simple brilliant insights crisscrossed both hemispheres of my brain and my life.

By 2006, Michael had successfully spun the entertainment division off from the radio and billboard parts of the giant Clear Channel Entertainment, which was based in Texas. We were now Live Nation, a name chosen to signify the global community of artists and fans that we served, a nation united in its love of music. This was a big time for us. No longer a small division on the balance sheet of a big media company, we were free to fulfill Michael's dream, the one he had drawn out on a napkin so many years before. We were the world's largest concert company, connecting artists and fans around the globe, with Michael as CEO. I was Michael's go-to guy, as I had been to the owner of the flea market, to Julio César Chávez, and to my Spanish-language concert company partner Ruben.

One day while sitting in my office, my daughter stopped by. Nataly was in high school then, which is a delicate time for fathers and daughters, a time when the relationship can often be summarized by, "Dad you embarrass the hell out me and drive me nuts. I really wish I lived somewhere else. Can I borrow the car? Oh, and $50?"

My daughter was becoming a woman and I was hanging on for dear life. While we were talking, Michael stopped by, as he often did as part of his hallway management style. He asked Nataly a few superficial questions and then he said something I couldn't believe. The truth is, I wanted to kill him at the time.

"Look Nataly. I'm going to tell you something that your father never will, but I can say it because I'm an outsider. We know you'll have sex, drink a bit, probably smoke pot. And you know how we know? Because we did it too when we were your age. What your dad really wants to teach you, he just doesn't know how, is not to make the big mistakes. Have sex, just be safe and don't get a disease or get pregnant before you're ready. Go to parties. Have fun. Just don't drink and drive or do hard drugs. Rebel. Push back. Just don't be stupid and hurt yourself. Okay?"

Nataly sat there dumbfounded. Then she smiled a smile of relief. As though Michael had in that one unrehearsed moment cleared up the angst and internal chaos she had been feeling. "Okay!" she said and gave him a hug.

Whoa! I couldn't believe what had just happened. Sex? Drinking? And the biggest surprise of all, that she hugged him. How had Michael managed to get a smile and a hug when all I got were snarls and slammed doors?

You see this was—is—his magic. Knowing exactly how to reach inside to find each person so he can connect with them.

One of my teachers later in life would tell me a story about a spiritual guru who walks into a warehouse and is fascinated by the forklift, admiring its ability to reach up and out and pick up things from many levels, always maintaining its center of gravity.

That is Michael Rapino.

* * *

Over the years I would be promoted many times. From COO of Touring to head of amphitheater programming to president of North American Concerts and, finally, to CEO of Global Music. I had become the executive I had set out to be, overseeing 15,000 concerts a year, 10,000 employees, and a billion dollars in revenue. I was an officer at a Fortune 500 company and that made me proud.

Learning to lead was trial by fire. I remember one particular vice president who worked for me ... or so I thought! I'll call him "The Battler."

The Battler was an odd man. He was a legend in the touring industry who looked nothing like the image you have in your mind of a concert promoter. He was a short man, always sniffling and wiping his nose. His complexion was eternally red, like an uncontained fire raged inside him— and it did. This fire expressed itself as an endless drive to work day and night, and as a complete inability to be told what to do.

His resumé, however, was that of a star. Decades of successful tours with Jimmy Buffett, Aerosmith, Britney Spears, 'N Sync, Backstreet Boys, and many more.

Managing The Battler, which I never really learned to do, was like fathering a brilliant teenager. It took a mix of strength, strategy, and the ability to surrender. Strength I had in spades. The strategy I was learning. Surrender … well it would be a long, long time before I learned that lesson.

At first I tried to sweet-talk him. I would be his friend, we would work together and everything would be kumbaya (or so I thought). But The Battler was a pro, a master manipulator who had been getting his way and working around his bosses while I was still selling gum in the schoolyard. He would call me into his office to counsel me on my management style. "Just bring everything to me and I'll help you," he'd say, "especially with whatever the other guys are working on … you have to be very careful with them."

Not feeling I was making a difference, I decided I would out-muscle him. Be a strong leader and lay down the law. That seemed to work well.

We would have great meetings and agree on the plan just as I'd said. Then he would leave the meeting and do exactly as he wanted, which was usually the opposite of whatever I said.

Like the time The Battler wanted to make a really big offer on a certain rock tour. I thought it was way too risky. After a lengthy meeting, we agreed not to make the offer. To soothe The Battler's ego, I offered to call the band's agent and explain our decision. Except when I called the agent, he laughed and said, "[The Battler] already made that offer last week!"

I was frustrated, feeling like I was failing. Determined to win, I pressed on through the obstacle course of the job.

My boss and mentor Michael would tell me to bring value to the team, not rules. "Help them get their job done and they will follow you," he said.

You see, what I failed to see at the time was that despite the fact The Battler wasn't following The Plan According To Jason—even though the path wasn't paved with gold and landscaped with roses—the results were great. We bought tours, sold tickets, and made money exactly as we were supposed to. Because I had been taught as a child to keep the peace and solve everyone's problems, I saw The Battler's independence as a sign that I was failing when in reality he and the entire division were producing and winning—they just did it their way. The more I tried to make it work my way, the more I would frustrate myself and fulfill my inner insecurities of not being good enough.

We had a habit of solving our issues on the outdoor patio of Michael's office. We sat around and battled back and forth like little kids while Michael calmly reviewed the facts and then decided how best to teach us each exactly what we needed to learn.

One day Michael recommended we read Jack Welch's new book, *Winning*. I went right out and bought it as I had done with every book he'd recommended to me since we first met.

A few weeks later we were sitting around the same table, discussing the same old problems disguised as new ones. As we talked, The Battler said, "You know that book you were talking about by Jack Welch?" I was surprised since I didn't think The Battler listened to anything anyone said, let alone a recommendation of what book to read.

"I read it," he said, "and there's a part in there that reminded me of Jason." He wiped his nose and recited the passage. "When you become a manager, you get a title not a crown."

In the moment it stung and I blindly defended myself with all my virtues and hard work. In retrospect, though, he was right. I was growing into my role as a manager, and like a child put in charge of his siblings for the first time, I was learning the hard way that being bossy isn't leadership.

Years later I would read and re-read the Tao Te Ching by Laozi, the father of Taoism. In one of those readings a passage grabbed my attention and reminded me of the early days of learning to govern.

"… The greatest conqueror wins without struggle. The most successful manager leads without dictating. This is intelligent non-aggressiveness.

This is called the mastery of men."

I smile often and remember fondly the lessons I learned from The Battler, the man I never truly managed, but who taught me so much about management.

Not all the lessons were as combative. Some were downright funny.

My first day as president of North American Concerts the phone rang; it was Sharon Osbourne. I had never met Sharon, but like everyone else on the planet I knew who she was—the Queen of Rock.

"Hi Jason," she said in her sweet voice. "I just wanted to call and say congratulations. And to make sure you are up for this job. It's a tough business, you know?"

Then she asked me a question that made me pause.

"Jason, if I were to tell you to go fuck yourself, what would you say?"

"Well Sharon," I said. "Today, not knowing you, I would probably just pretend I didn't hear you. But give me some time, once we're friends, and I'll tell ya to fuck off right back ... and then we can get down to business."

Sharon laughed. "You're going to do just fine," she said.

A couple of hours later a giant fruit basket arrived with a note from Sharon. It said simply, "Fuck you Jason. Much Love, Sharon."

* * *

Along the way there were many accomplishments of which I am very proud—record growth; budgets reached and surpassed; a united team working to win together; over 100,000 concerts produced by my divisions. And always Michael, driving me to be the best Jason I could be. As I said, plenty to be proud of. Looking back, though, I'm most touched by the personal moments.

Michael was a wise, caring man teaching his young student. In the end, that's what a guru is. In that respect Michael was my first guru. Yeah, he was in an office instead of an ashram and he wore a collared shirt instead of a robe, and had PowerPoint slides instead of a tattered book of teachings. But in all the ways that counted, he was my guru.

There is one final lesson from Michael, a recent, real-life lesson that summarizes what this book is all about. The point I made in the introduction—that we can change the world from our desks. That enlightenment can look like you and me.

As I was writing this book I got a Google Alert for Live Nation. I always follow the company's progress, rooting silently from the sidelines like a soccer mom on a school field.

I opened the alert expecting a new artist signing or news of their expansion into a new city somewhere on the globe. Instead there was a headline and a quote that brought a tear to my eye and smile to my heart. It reinforced everything I have learned and exemplified, that all of us can change the world through everyday enlightened acts.

The headline read:

Live Nation to Serve Locally-Grown Produce, Meat from Responsibly-Raised Animals and New Vegetarian Options in its North American Amphitheaters

It was followed by this quote from my friend and mentor:

"I know in my own home it is important for my family to buy locally-grown produce, to know where our meat comes from, and to have a variety of vegetarian options whenever possible ... So we felt as a company that we should be able to deliver the same quality to our millions of fans ...."

To me, this truly was enlightenment in action, a demonstration that it's possible to bring more joy, more love, and more compassion to the planet from any chair in which you find yourself sitting. Michael's announcement was a reinforcement of what I was coming to believe ... that enlightenment isn't only for people wearing robes or living in ashrams who can sit perfectly still and meditate with a clear mind for hours on end; we can all raise the frequency of the world around us in the day-to-day decisions we make as executives, fathers, mothers, lovers, friends, and neighbors.

One more lesson in leadership and life from my CEO ... my guru.

·*10*·

THE PORN STAR, COLDPLAY, AND THE MISSING MUSTACHE

IT WAS AUGUST 2005 AND I KNOCKED TIMIDLY ON THE DRESSING ROOM door at the Air Canada Center in Toronto. Chris Martin, the front man of the hottest band in the world at the time, Coldplay, opened the door and looked at me, no doubt wondering about the young man holding four handycams. I introduced myself.

"Hi Chris, I'm Jason Garner from Live Nation ... and, um, I'll be on tour with you. We have a gift for you ... these cameras ... so you and the guys can film mementos from the tour. Anyway, I just wanted to tell you that anything you need ... that's what I'm here for ... ."

Without missing a beat he smiled slyly and said, "Thanks for the cameras. If you want to do something for me, shave that mustache. You look like a '70's porn star." Then he smiled again and shut the door.

I stood there dumbfounded, not sure what to say or do. Their manager, my friend Dave, walked up and I told him what happened. He laughed and said not to worry. He told me that Chris was joking and I should get used to it.

I had spent the latter part of 2004 working with my new boss Michael on this tour. It was really his tour and his relationship, but I was here on the road. I had spent my career up until then with Hispanic acts, explaining to my English-speaking friends and family who they were. Not any more; I was out with Coldplay, mustache and all.

The mustache to which Chris was referring had been growing since high school. I always had a bit of a baby face and I was desperate to look more mature and to be taken seriously. So I grew out my mustache. I loved it and there was no way I was going to shave it. Not even for Coldplay.

I would spend the next year and a half on the road with the band. Traveling from city to city, hotel to hotel, venue to venue. It was a great experience and a good opportunity to meet the Live Nation teams that worked in each city. It was a job, an education, and a dream-come-true all rolled in one.

I remember one night traveling from one city to the next. We were flying in a Boeing Business Jet, which is like flying in your own living room. We were all sitting around watching the Rob Reiner movie *This Is Spinal Tap!*, laughing and telling jokes. Chris grabbed a chocolate bar and took a bite. Then, realizing I was sitting next to him, he broke off a piece and gave it to me. It was a simple gesture from a rock star to his young promoter to help me feel at home.

At the end of August, the tour brought me home to Los Angeles. It was a relief to be home and to see my family, and to host the band in the city where our company was headquartered.

I organized a dinner backstage at the Verizon Wireless Amphitheater on the first night of our two-show run. My boss Michael, Dave the manager, and Chris and his wife, Gwyneth Paltrow, were there in what was one of the biggest pinch-myself moments of my young life.

Chris told Michael how happy he and the band were. Everything was going great. The team on the road was wonderful. And ... "Jason is like part of the family."

I just beamed. What more could possibly happen? This was amazing.

Chris went on: "I only really have one complaint. Something that shouldn't be a problem to solve. Something simple."

"What Chris?" Michael said.

"It's that damn mustache of Jason's. I've been asking him to shave it. He told me he was here to make us happy. Anything we asked ... but he won't shave the mustache."

The whole table laughed. I cringed inside, but laughed on the outside and played along.

The concert was a huge success, every seat filled with an ecstatic fan, just like the entire global tour.

After the show I headed back to the hotel where I was staying with the band. I went to my room to prepare for bed. When I looked in the mirror I saw the mustache. "Wouldn't it be funny if ... ." I thought. "No, I can't." I debated with myself. Then I picked up my electric razor, closed my eyes, and ... .

The next day I came downstairs early, before our lobby call. I positioned myself right in front of the elevators, my naked face smiling. The door opened and out walked Chris. His jaw dropped, his eyes opened wide ... and then he let out a laugh that made it all worth it.

My favorite rock star story. Looking back, Chris was right. The truth is the mustache *did* make me look like a '70s porn star.

·*11*·

TOBY KEITH, I LOVE THAT SWEATER

IN MARCH 2006 I HAD A DAY OFF FROM THE COLDPLAY TOUR AFTER A sold-out concert in Washington D.C. I checked the calendar to see what other Live Nation shows were in the area and saw that Toby Keith was playing at Mohegan Sun in Uncasville, Connecticut.

I called our president of Nashville, Brian, to see if I should come. He said yes. So I made the arrangements to get there from DC and was on my way.

Brian, or BOC as he is affectionately known, was more than the president of our Nashville operation, he was a star himself. Looking the part of a country promoter, he's tall and blonde with designer jeans and expensive boots. He travels the roads of America 40 weeks a year in a tour bus complete with satellite TV so he won't miss a college football or Chicago Cubs game. He promotes the tours of nearly the entire country music industry: Toby, Brooks & Dunn, Rascal Flatts, Brad Paisley, Tim McGraw, and so many more. He is their promoter, their friend, and part of the gang.

I had been on tour with Coldplay for quite some time. My standard attire, in keeping with the band and crew, was jeans and a black T-shirt.

In preparing to go to see Toby Keith, I looked for something a bit more "country," whatever that means. I really had no idea what to wear. To make matters worse, it was snowing in Connecticut. I shuffled through my suitcase. I finally found something warm and settled on jeans, a white T-shirt, and an olive green button-up cardigan sweater. I don't know why but it made sense at the time.

I had never met Toby Keith before. He had a reputation for being a practical joker, a good ol' boy. I felt some of that high school insecurity creep in. I was suddenly the new kid facing a crowd of cool kids. I tried to put it out of my mind. After all, I was an executive with the largest concert company in the world. He would be proud to meet me. Right?

Getting to Uncasville wasn't easy in the snow. The trip was a combination of train and car service, and was a slow-go in the inclement weather. I was tired and starting to regret the decision. But it was my job and I was looking forward to seeing my friend Brian, and meeting Toby.

I arrived at the venue a little before show time. I was shown back to a large room where Toby was doing some meet-and-greets for a sponsor. I stood in the corner near the door and watched him joke and play with his fans, making them feel right at home.

Then, without warning, it happened. He spotted me. Not that he knew who I was, but he spotted me nonetheless. In a voice that caused the entire room to stop and stare, he bellowed:

"Son, what in the *fuck* are you wearing??!!"

For a split second I thought about making a run for it. A who's who of the country live entertainment industry was glaring at me—green sweater, red face, looking as out of place as I had years earlier in Julio César Chávez's dressing room.

But I did what I'd always done. I made the best of it. I smiled and said, "I wore it just for you. Don't you like it?"

That green sweater would become a longstanding joke.

The next play was mine. When Brian and Toby took their next trip to Iraq and Afghanistan to support the troops, I bought five green sweaters, wrapped them up, and shipped them off with a note:

"Thought you could use some camouflage."

The joke didn't end there. A few years later I hosted a meeting for the Live Nation North American promoter team, which was a celebration of a record-breaking year. We had arranged for the Jonas Brothers, at the height of their success, to perform live. Each of our tour promoters sent in videos of their artist clients congratulating the team on a job well done.

I thought I knew the contents of the video montage. There I stood on stage, the proud leader, sharing messages of support with his team. Then a familiar voice and a familiar message ....

"Hi Live Nation. This is Toby Keith. Jason Garner, what was he thinking wearing a green cardigan to a country show?!"

From this, a simple lesson: sometimes life's biggest embarrassments turn out to be the greatest stories.

·*12*·

LEARNING TO BREATHE

IN THE SUMMER OF 2006 I WAS IN NEW YORK ON BUSINESS. I USED TO LIKE to say that, because it made me sound and feel like the businessmen I'd seen in movies growing up. There's something about walking down the streets of New York, bustling from meeting to meeting, that makes even the most seasoned businessman feel accomplished.

I was walking into a meeting at a talent agency when my phone rang. The caller ID said UNAVAILABLE, which I assumed meant it was my family calling from Mexico. They had gone to visit my then-wife's family in her hometown outside Guadalajara.

I answered the phone to hear my wife screaming. At first I couldn't make out anything. The reception was horrible and she was screaming so loudly that the result was a garbled mix of sounds. Finally I heard her say, "Kevin ... shot ... dead." And the phone cut out.

I stood there paralyzed. My heart was in my throat. I tried frantically to call her back, but each time I tried I got a message saying the call wouldn't go through. All I could think was that my son was dead.

For the next 30 minutes I dialed that number. Dial ... no luck ... dial again ... no luck ... again ... nothing ... come on ... again ... no ... again and again ... desperately trying ... clinging to hope that I had misunderstood, the only thing keeping me upright and dialing was the adrenaline that was winning the internal battle with the utter devastation and panic I felt. Dial ... nothing ... re-dial ... no ... dial ... oh my God, my poor little boy ... what am I going to do?

I began trying numbers of her family members. Finally I reached my brother-in-law and he gave me the news.

My son was alive. But there *had* been a killing. My father-in-law had been shot and killed. My son was with him, next to him when it happened and was the only witness. The family was in shock.

I booked the first flight I could, JFK to LAX and then to Guadalajara. I rushed to the airport. No time to think let alone process what had happened.

I got to the airport, checked in, sat down in the lounge and I fell apart.

A month later Kevin and I sat together, still reeling from the tragic event, waiting to see the therapist I had hired to help Kevin deal with his emotions. A few moments later Dr. Vera Dunn emerged.

She was pencil thin and had a warm smile, a blonde Susan Sarandon. Vera greeted us and we walked downstairs to the office in the basement of her Beverly Hills home.

We spoke for a moment. I recounted the details of the shooting. How Kevin had gone for a ride with my father-in-law at his cattle ranch; that along the way they encountered a former employee who had returned drunk to the ranch seeking revenge; how my father-in-law confronted him and asked him to leave. The gunfire. A shot through the windshield inches above Kevin's head. My father-in-law's stomach wound. How he fell to the ground before the gunman walked over and icily shot him in the head—while my son watched.

Vera worked intensely with Kevin for a few months, and then off and on after that. Children's minds are so magical. With her help he was able to put the event in a box and resolve it in a way that allowed him to grow into the amazing young man he is today.

* * *

In late 2008 my second marriage ended. Another stab at love and another failure. Maybe I'm just not cut out for marriage, I thought at the time.

I was a single father for the second time in my life, and the irony that I was somehow re-playing my mom's love life wasn't lost on me. In fact it scared the shit out of me.

I needed help. So I called the only person I could think of: Vera.

There I was sitting in the waiting room again, waiting for Vera to come up the stairs like she had two years earlier with Kevin. After a life succeeding at about everything I had ever set my mind to, I had failed not once, but twice, at marriage. I felt horrible. Worse still, I had put my kids through the love rollercoaster just like my mom had with my sister and me. UGGGHHH.

Sitting with Vera I told her all the reasons my marriage had failed. We were too young. It wasn't right. She did this and that. I'm married to my job and no one understands me. Blah. Blah. Blah.

Then I explained to Vera how she could best work with me. I thought I knew myself so well that I didn't want Vera to waste any time doing the things she did with her other clients. I would give her special instructions so this would be quick and painless and I could get on with my life.

She looked at me kindly. She smiled knowingly, like a woman who had done this many times before. And then she said simply, "Take a deep breath."

Okay, that's easy. In and out. What's next?

"Try it again, only this time breathe in deeply through your mouth. Fill your chest as much as you can, and then exhale with abandon. Just let the air flow out," she said, still smiling kindly.

So I did. Hmm. That felt weird.

"Try it five times in a row now, Jason. Nice, long, breaths," Vera gently prodded me on.

Inhale...hold...exhale. One. Inhale...hold...exhale.... Two. What's that feeling? Inhale...hold...exhale.... Three. Feeling flush, I started to sense something, like a wave starting at my toes, moving through my legs, now sitting in the pit of my stomach.

"Nice, Jason. Keep going," Vera's gentle voice reminded me.

Inhale... hold... exhale. Four. Now the wave was sitting in my throat. Sitting isn't quite the right word. It was swelling, and I had an inkling of what was coming next. Inhale ... hold ... exhale. With that last breath I let out a sob, a verbal expression of all the years of fear and insecurity. I gasped for air. Then I wailed. I cried for what felt like an hour. Every inch of my body was shaking. The pain stored in my body was released, excruciatingly, cell by cell. All the emotion I had repressed and hidden behind the mask of Super Jason was now being released.

As I caught my breath, Vera looked at me. She smiled while her eyes silently spoke to me. "*I understand. I know. I'm here,*" they said.

Then Vera spoke softly, "Jason, I am here for you. We will do this together. You are loved."

I breathed ... and then I cried some more.

·13·

MY MOM

ON MY FIRST DAY OF KINDERGARTEN I CRIED. I MISSED MY MOM AND I felt all alone despite being in a class filled with 30 children. So I cried. I actually remember this, mainly because a little girl, whose name I don't recall, raised her hand. The teacher called on her and she said, "He's crying," pointing at me. Then I was sad AND embarrassed.

I don't remember crying much in my life after that. I don't think I had time. No pause button on the rocket ship up to the executive desk at Live Nation.

That all changed when I started to see Vera regularly.

It's amazing what happens when you breathe. Not the shallow breathing most of us do as we rush through life. But true, deep, fill-your-chest breaths.

It's as if there are pockets of feelings stored up inside and with every few breaths you hit one of those pockets and bring feelings to the surface. Then you cry. The thing is, these pockets of emotion are attached to past events, things you don't remember when you were a little kid. So when you cry, you cry like a child, as though the little you is feeling that pain all over again. Like your first big bowel movement after being constipated and taking a laxative, it sucks, but it's liberating and you aren't sure if it's ever going to stop!

I started seeing Vera twice a week. I realized after that first big cry that I needed help. Dealing with a divorce, running a division of a Fortune 500 company and raising two kids ... I was drowning. Vera was my life raft.

We sketched my immediate family tree on a dry-erase board as part of my therapy. On it were my grandma and grandpa on each side, my mom and dad, their brothers and sisters, and then my sister and me and our spouses and children.

Vera explained that our concept of ourselves, the story that governs our life, is formed beginning in the womb before we have any idea of anything, while our brain is empty, like a blank chalkboard. We begin to get impulses from our moms. Millions and millions of impulses each day. We feel everything mommy feels AND we even feel the things she doesn't realize she's feeling. This becomes our concept of the world, our primary scenario.

Vera compared this to a pair of tinted glasses through which we observe the world. I think it's even more pervasive than that. It *is* our world, skewing everything we see and experience.

I think of that world like a can of paint. When we are conceived the can is filled with white paint; this is our brain. Then we start getting impulses from our moms. With each impulse a squirt of color goes into the can. She gets scared, a squirt of black. She gets angry, a squirt of red. Dad comes home late, a squirt of green. Millions upon millions upon millions of impulses turning into colors.

By the time we're born our can of white paint is a dark swirl of all of mom's emotions. That is our world. There is no more seeing our world as white, because it isn't. So we live in a tinted world, the colored world taught to us silently by our moms.

This isn't to blame moms or to say that all the feelings are negative. Our moms experienced all kinds of feelings. All kinds of emotions. But most of our moms were young and scared and unprepared for the massive challenges of pregnancy and childbirth.

Our moms were also dealing with their own paint cans, filled with impulses from their mothers. They did their best, but all the impulses tinted their paint cans too. All of it formed our world.

Then we are born. Our little eyes open and we see the world for the first time, we hear through our ears, we touch through our fingers. But those eyes and ears and fingers are all connected to our brain, our paint can. And so as we grow, we believe that we're independent from our moms; rebelliously different. But we're not; we are a swirl of paint colors.

This is why, despite all the perceived differences in our lives, my grandma, mom, and I all ended up alone, raising children, feeling misunderstood. Because we had one thing in common above all else: we shared the same paint can.

This is the purpose of the dry-erase board, to retrace the family history and better understand the family story—or filter—that has been passed down through the generations.

Vera asked me to recount my story, starting with my grandma.

My grandmother, June, was the oldest of three children. She and her two brothers, whose names I will never know, lived with their mom and dad. Her dad was an alcoholic and her mom … well, she was a woman who one night went out into the snow to buy some milk and never came home. She died in an icy accident.

So one morning my little nine-year-old grandma awoke to learn that her mommy was dead. This could be a sad story with a happy ending, one in which her dad cleans up, fathers his children, and they learn to live and love. But it's not.

My grandma's dad planted himself on a bar stool and drank away his pain. When I say he planted himself on a bar stool I mean that literally. He sat on that stool and drank for so many days, and weeks, and months, and years that many years later the last story of her family my grandma would hear is that her dad died, on that bar stool with a glass in his hand and a broken heart.

He left June and her brothers to fend for themselves. With no time to mourn the loss of her mother, my grandmother inherited the role of mom and lost her childhood. She cared for her brothers night and day. When her youngest brother ran out into the chilly snow at night looking for his mommy, it was little June who collected him and put him to sleep.

She had found, by necessity, a place of love to care for her two little brothers, where the pain of death didn't reside. But that didn't last too long. Soon the state heard of this situation and they came to investigate. They did what states do and rescued the children from this nightmare. Except the nightmare got worse.

In those days orphanages were segregated. There were homes for boys and homes for girls. So after that day, my grandma never saw her brothers again. In a matter of months, little June had lost everything that mattered—her mom, her dad, her brothers, her home.

Sitting on the wood floor of the orphanage she did what any child dying of a broken heart would do. She turned off her heart and locked it in a safe place where no one would ever hurt her again.

"Wow," Vera said. "Are you starting to see how your grandma's story played a role in who you are?" She continued: "So now we know Grandma June's story. How do you think she felt?"

Scared. Really scared. She probably felt unloved, alone, and not good enough, like the world was against her. I remember my grandma telling me a story about the ladies at the orphanage offering her a doll. She refused because she didn't want to give them the satisfaction of seeing her smile. I think the truth is she didn't take it because if she allowed herself to feel love it would have opened the floodgates of grief and despair that she had bottled up inside.

"Now," Vera said. "What would her daughter have felt, your mom?"

Well, my grandma was afraid to hold her, to cuddle her, to nurture her. She thought she would break her. So I'm sure my mom felt unlovable, scared, not good enough. All alone without a mommy to comfort her.

"See the pattern, Jason? Keep going, what else would she have felt?"

I remember my mom always working really hard, my entire childhood, to support my sister Onne and me. And she was always giving to the world. Always giving. All the time. To everyone. It was as though my mom was a saint and a martyr all wrapped into one. She was a woman full of love and tenderness. Not a day went by, no matter how tired or frustrated or exhausted to the bone she was, that we didn't get hugs. Not one or two but lots of hugs. In fact she had an endless supply of hugs for us and for every other child with whom she came into contact.

My mom worked three jobs when I was in grade school. In the morning she dropped Onne and me at school then drove a few miles to the Chandler Tripp School for severely disabled children, where she was an aide. My mom loved children and the more they needed her, the better. She poured her heart out and loved them with everything she had.

At Chandler Tripp she did exhausting work in the swimming pool with children who could barely sit up in a wheelchair. She moved their arms and legs and supported them while they moved around in the water. This was just the beginning of her day. By lunchtime she would arrive at my school, where she worked as an aide in my classroom. When the regular school day ended she would take my sister and me with her to a nearby day-care center where she finished the day working as a teacher. My sister and I tried our best to be good children, get our homework done, and not get in the way while my mom took care of other people's kids.

I remember waiting with my sister, dying to get home, while my mom hugged a never-ending line of children as they were picked up by their parents. It was the highlight of these kids' day ... a hug and a sticker from Grandma Sue-Sue, as she was called.

"Exactly. Now, Jason, what would the son of a mother who was the daughter of Grandma June have felt? What did little Jason feel?" Vera asked this with tender eyes.

Before I could speak the words I cried again. It was another good, long, uncontrolled cry like the first session with Vera.

Little Jason—little me—felt scared. He felt he had to be perfect. He had to work and work and help and help. He felt alone, and so he became super human. Nothing could stop him. Because he believed if he reached a certain place, a high enough level, he would be loved. And if he didn't he would end up like his mom and grandma ... unloved.

Then I cried some more as my whole life became clear. The endless hard work, the obsessive drive to the top, the stubborn refusal to be less than the best. All of it was a subconscious attempt by the little boy in me to find love and safety and security.

With the tone of a nurturing mother, Vera gently brought the day to a close. "Your grandma's tragic story was passed down to your mom, in the way all of our generational themes are. Without words, through thought after thought, impulse after impulse, and feeling upon feeling of fear and insecurity. Each time your grandma cringed at the thought of picking up her tiny girl she transported your mom back to that orphanage where she sat all alone so many years before. That's the same feeling you had, Jason, years later sitting alone at the day-care center trying to be a good boy so your mommy would notice you."

It all started in the desperate mind of my nine-year-old orphaned grandma and now had come full circle through the generations, down to me.

* * *

A month or so into my therapy, I got a phone call. I was in the shower. I jumped out, hurriedly grabbed a towel, and ran for the phone. I was waiting for this call.

Several weeks earlier doctors had found a lump in my mom's stomach. She had gone for a biopsy and we were awaiting the results.

"Hello?"

"Hi Bubs." It was my sister. Bubs was a nickname she'd had for me since she was a small child unable to say brother.

She paused, just long enough—in a way I will never forget—that I knew what she was going to say before the words came through the phone.

"Mom has cancer. Stage 4 ..." and then she cried.

I don't remember the rest of the call. The next thing I remember was being back in the shower. I was washing myself. Out of breath. Then I realized: "Jason, you even work hard in the shower. You can stop now. Your mom is dying. Who will be proud of you now?"

I fell to the shower floor and cried, screaming out. The little boy in me was exhausted from a life of subconsciously seeking love, and now overwhelmed by the realization that his mom, the woman whose love he had desperately sought, was dying.

I went to see Vera the next day. I told her the news. I told her what happened in the shower. I was scared. I was falling apart. How was I supposed to keep moving forward with all this going on? Why did I feel like I was the one who was dying?

In answer to my questions, Vera pulled out the dry-erase board with my family written on it. She took out a red pen and put an X through my ex-wife's name, whom I had recently divorced. She put a red X through my dad's name, as I'd had no contact with him for decades. Then she put a red X through my mom's name. Suddenly, my name on the board was all alone, just like I felt at that moment and just like I had felt so many times throughout my life.

I thought I had cried before, but nothing compared to this cry. It came from somewhere beyond my physical body, as if I was sobbing for my entire family. For my little orphaned grandma, for my little unloved mom, and for me. Especially for me.

I looked at Vera. She put her arm on my shoulder and told me, "This will get better, Jason. We will find the light."

In that difficult moment, the stubborn, nothing-can-stop-me spirit that had defined my life reappeared and, through the tears, I said, "We fucking better, Vera."

I had told and retold the story of Jason Garner throughout my life. I was making up new versions as frequently as I needed to surmount the challenges I faced. But nothing had prepared me for this. I was facing something different. Far more personal. I was cracking open my soul, getting to know myself. The real me. And in the middle of it all, my mom was dying.

* * *

It was mid-July 2009. Onne, my mom's wife Kim, my grandma June, and I were sitting in the living room of my mom's house. My mom, in the last stages of her life, was lying on the couch. The pain of the cancerous tumor growing inside her had increased, as had the dosages of medication she was taking to relieve it. This gave us precious few moments in each day when she was fully present and not loopy from the medication.

My grandma's hands trembled. In them she held a few sheets of binder paper and some handwritten notes. More than notes, they were the first-ever, true expressions of her heart, the peeling open of the story she had locked away seventy years earlier sitting alone in the orphanage.

We sat there holding our breath, not sure what to expect. Everyone but me, I knew what was written on those scraps of paper.

A few days earlier, realizing that our mom didn't have much time left, my sister and I talked about how to make this experience as meaningful as possible for our children, my mom's grandkids. Instead of the next couple of weeks being a time of fear, shutting down and hiding their emotions, how could we turn it into something deeply meaningful that would strengthen their bond with their grandma and help them, help us all, tap into the deep love we shared?

We decided that we and the kids would write her letters. This was our plan to make sure of two things. First, that nothing went unsaid. All the things that were too hard to say face-to-face would be written down. It would be a chance to express everything in our hearts. And second, the part we didn't tell the kids yet, that the connection with their grandma would actually grow through this process because they would read the letters to her.

We all spent the next few days writing, crying, expressing. Finally, when the letters were finished, we met at my mom's house. The children thought we were meeting there to give Grandma a hug and hand her the letters. They were wrong.

I stood up and smiled at the kids. I had butterflies in my stomach because I knew what they didn't. I held my letter in my hand and said simply, "I'll go first." Then I turned and walked into the room where my mom was resting.

Watching your mom slowly die is unlike any other experience. It's as if a part of you is slowly pulled from inside. From deep inside your intestines. Day by day. Bit by bit. It's agonizing. Painful like no other experience. Right in the middle of your gut. A deep, slow, painful ache.

I sat down on the bed. I held her hand. I cried, just as I cry right now remembering. There is no holding back tears or being strong in moments like that. It's life, playing out in the raw. Naked and real.

Then I told her what we were going to do, that each of us had written her a letter. That it was our intention nothing go unsaid. That we end this day 100% certain that she knew exactly how we felt about her. That together, through this experience and honest expression, we would grow. Even as her life slipped away, the love would grow stronger.

She looked at me. There was a deep desperation in her eyes. And she said honestly, "I don't know if I can do this, Jason."

"Yes, mom, you can. All you have to do is lie there and listen. You don't have to take care of us anymore. It's our turn. We are all hurting inside. You can't fix that, so don't try. Just accept our love. That's all that's left to do."

Her eyes softened. Then they filled with tears. A lifetime of taking care of the world, of desperately trying to keep us from pain, of trying to prevent the kinds of feelings we were all experiencing right then, all melted away in that moment.

"Okay, J," she said. She gently squeezed my hand, the way she had when I was growing up to tell me everything was all right.

And I cried. Just like that little boy had cried so many times. All the scared nights and uncertain times. All the fights with my mom as I expanded into manhood. All the pushing away, while secretly longing to be held. In that moment it was all okay. Perfect. Just me and my mom. And my letter .... .

So I read, interrupted by the frequent sobs that erupted from us both. I should have saved that letter. I didn't think to, but I do remember the last few lines.

"I spent my entire life trying to be a good boy. I worked so hard, achieved so much, all of it to make my mommy proud. And now, surrounded by so much stuff, a fancy title, a nice house, a great job, everything I thought I always wanted ... I realize I would trade it all ... every last bit ... for one more day with my mom."

I fell into her arms in a way I hadn't for many years. Perhaps ever. The way a baby does when it falls asleep on its mother's chest. And I cried. We cried.

When I sat up I noticed a twinkle in my mom's eyes. Behind the tears, there was joy. "I love you my son," she said.

When I emerged from the room my face was stained by the tracks of tears I had cried, which told the children everything they needed to know. Silently they got up, one by one, walked into that room, and read their letters to their dying grandma. And one by one they emerged. Crying. Sad. But also a little closer to the woman they so loved.

On the drive back to my sister's house later that afternoon we sat quietly, knowing we had both experienced something deeply important. For ourselves, for our children, and for our mom.

"What about Nana?" I asked my sister, referring to Grandma June.

"Oh no," my sister said. "Remember the last time we tried to get them to open up?"

I did. A few days prior we had encouraged my mom and grandma to talk about their feelings, to unravel the complicated relationship that bound them together. The conversation had lasted about two minutes before my mom, nearing death and therefore finally free of the need to please her mother, told my grandma to leave.

"We have to figure this out," I told my sister. "I'll talk to Nana."

My grandma had always had trouble bonding with women. I think now it was probably a deep anger that lived inside her. The feelings of a little girl who was mad at her mommy for dying, for leaving her all alone. This was the anger she carried with her and that was expressed to the women in her life whom she loved.

That, unfortunately, often meant that my mom and my sister could do little right in the eyes of my grandma. If they called too often, they were told to stop smothering her. If they didn't call enough, they were told they had abandoned her. If they asked a question she didn't like, they got a stern look and sassy response. They spent their time subconsciously trying to mend my grandma's broken heart. And she wouldn't let them.

As if to make it just a little more difficult, my relationship with Nana was the opposite. I could do no wrong. If I didn't call her for a month, it was all erased with a "Hey Nana" and a smile. She adored me. She understood me. I understood her. Even before I learned the emotional reality of what brewed inside her. I just knew.

So I went to see my Nana. I arrived at her apartment in the assisted living complex. I knocked on her door. No answer. This, to the facility staff and everyone else, was a sign that Grandma June wanted to be left alone. To me it just meant that my crabby granny needed a hug. In I walked.

She was in her underwear, sitting in a purple armchair my sister and I had given her.

"Ha ha ha," She laughed with a bellow. "Well Bucko, you caught me with my drawers down!"

I stepped back outside while she put on something more appropriate, then came back in a few moments later.

"How's your mom today?" she asked me.

I noted a tinge of guilt about her failed attempt to talk to her daughter a few days before. So I didn't waste any time.

"Nana." I reached out and held my grandma's hand. I began to cry.

"Oh, don't cry, J," she pleaded. "I can't bear any more crying. This is all so hard."

This was the side of my grandma that most people never saw. The scared girl trying to keep it all together.

"Nana. My mom, your daughter, is dying. I don't know how much time we have left. A few days, or a week. Not long. And then that's it. We won't see her again." I paused to wipe my tears and gauge the effect on my grandma. She looked at me knowingly. So I continued.

"What happened the other day. You and her. That can't happen ever again. There can be no more fighting."

"Well … ." She started to interrupt me and then she stopped.

"None of it matters anymore," I said. "All that matters is the love in your heart. The love you haven't shared. You know exactly what she needs to hear … and what you need to say."

My grandma cried like I had never seen her cry before. She nodded at me to say she understood.

"Today," I told her, "we all read letters to mom. Letters telling her everything we felt. Our love. Our regrets. Our hopes and our fears. We didn't hold back. Now you have to do the same, Nana … you have to. Tomorrow is the last chance."

We held each other and cried. Two people having a conversation only they could.

"I'll pick you up at ten tomorrow morning," I said.

I kissed her and got up to leave, then I turned one more time before opening the door. Before I could speak, my grandma said firmly, "I know, J ... ."

The next day in the car we didn't speak much. She clenched three pieces of paper in her hands. At stoplights and stop signs I employed a skill I had learned as a concert promoter, a skill an old-time talent agent had taught me: reading upside down, sideways, from any and all angles.

"Jason," Chris had said. "The most important thing you can do is learn to read upside down. Most people won't look you in the eye when they talk to you. So when you walk into their office and they start babbling about something or other, you just listen. While you're listening you look down at their desk and read away. You'll be amazed at what you'll learn. And you'll thank me one day."

What I saw on those papers amazed me. My grandma had bared her soul. She had opened up in a way I couldn't believe. It was perfect. As I drove to my mom's house, I smiled.

When we arrived we all sat down. My mom was lying on the couch just as she'd been the last time the two women had tried to talk. My sister and Kim had told my mom what was going on and my mom had reluctantly agreed. Lying there, she looked at me with a "this better be worth it" look that only your mom can give you.

My grandma's hands trembled. She stared at the papers intensely, almost as if wishing she could escape between their lines to avoid this difficult situation. She cleared her throat and began.

"I know that you have never understood me ... ."

Oh shit. Here we go again.

My mom quickly spoke up. "I can't do this again. I won't."

With my left hand I touched my grandma. With my right I rubbed my mom's shoulder. My sister and Kim hugged my mom and told her it was okay.

Grandma continued.

"That's because I haven't been honest with you. I have hidden so much from everyone, from myself."

Her hands were shaking and the shaking had traveled to her lips. But she didn't cry … no, she was too tough for that, just as she'd been too tough to take the doll offered to her in the orphanage. She wasn't going to lose it here. She had come that day to speak her peace. To say what she knew needed to be said. She had made a list of her truths and she read them … one by one.

"A few days before my mom died in that accident, I was baking with her. We were making a cake. We made the batter together, mixing the ingredients, having a great time. When it came time to put the cake in the oven she told me I couldn't help. I was hurt. She was just trying to keep me safe from the hot oven but I didn't understand. So I got mad. My mom sent me to my room, and in my room I sat there fuming. Furious. And then … ."

She paused, a pause that cut through the room. Silent yet so profound it almost had sound. "And then," Grandma June went on, "I said over and

116

over and over again ... I hope you die mommy ... I hate you."

It was as if a giant vacuum had sucked the air out of the room. We just sat there. Stunned.

But Grandma June didn't notice. She went on with her list. "When you were a baby I didn't hold you. I was sure I would break you. I couldn't remember anyone holding me and I didn't think I knew how. I'm really sorry for that. I know how it made you feel. I know how it affected you. Maybe this cancer ... maybe it's because of that ...."

My mom burst. Like a water balloon plucked by a tiny needle, she burst. She lunged to grab hold of her mother's hand. She squeezed with all the power she had left, holding on with the little life that still resided in her and all the love of a little girl whose mommy had finally told her that she loved her.

"No, mother," she said. But before she could say more my grandma marched on.

"When you married the children's father, I knew I should talk to you. I knew I should tell you certain things, but I was too scared. I was scared you wouldn't listen. That you would reject me. I didn't want to feel that again ...." Another pause. She gulped down hard. "I didn't want to feel like I had when no one cared about me as a girl. So I didn't say anything. Then I watched you suffer with him. And I have never forgiven myself."

My mom groaned from deep inside. A release from every cell in her body. She sobbed, unable to believe what she was hearing.

"I haven't ever said this before," my grandma went on, oblivious to what was going on around her. "And I want you to know, I'm happy you are my daughter. I love you, Sue."

I don't remember a single word after that. The truth is, nothing else mattered. My grandma had finally spoken the truth, a truth that had haunted our family. The unspoken story that had traveled from that orphanage in Minnesota to my mom's living room in San Jose. The truth that had become a tumor. The pain that had caused that tumor to grow and grow and sap my mom's life. And now, finally, the untold fears of an abandoned nine-year-old girl had finally been expressed, and our family would never be the same.

I spent a long time feeling the tragedy of this moment. How devastatingly sad it was that a mom and a daughter had lived their whole lives without ever truly knowing each other. How tragic, that it took death to bring them together. The horrible irony of true love arriving just as life passed on.

While writing this essay, and then reading it to my wife, I had a new perspective. One that leapt from me with the same groan my mom made when my grandma read her that list.

My mom had spent her whole life teaching others to love. From the disabled children in the swimming pool to the kids waiting in line for a hug from Grandma Sue-Sue, to the animals she rescued on the side of the road. She taught them to love.

During the last few days of my mom's life, before the talk with my grandma, she would often talk about seeing a little girl. Occasionally she would cry and point. "I need to take care of the little girl, she needs me." We dismissed this at the time as hallucinations from a dying soul.

But now thinking back, perhaps on her deathbed, my mom—with that last bit of life she was clinging to—had one final mission. Her true life's mission, to teach little June ... the orphaned girl, her mommy, the young girl who needed her ... how to love. In doing so, she taught us all.

* * *

On the morning of July 18 my mom passed. Lying in the arms of her wife, daughter, and son, her chest rattled its last breath.

I had spent that night sleeping with her in her bed. I'd asked Kim if this would be okay with her. Kim had so selflessly cared for my mom, so defined the word wife, that I laugh now when I hear the debates about gay marriage. The world would be blessed if every wife were like Kim.

Like every loving wife and mother would, Kim said yes. I knew she wanted to be with my mom. It was probably my mom's last night, we all knew that. But Kim also wanted me to be okay.

So I climbed into bed. My mom was barely conscious, her chest rattling. I struggle now to describe the sound. Those of you who have heard it know what I'm talking about. It's a wet gargle, as if from deep inside a dark cave, a haunting sound. A deathly reminder that my mom was taking her last breaths, a sound so horrible it made me long for the end I so dreaded.

I tried to sleep but couldn't. Maybe it was the rattling or maybe it was just the knowing that I wouldn't see my mom again.

I've never told anyone this before: I spent that night talking with my mom in between her doses of morphine. I just talked. There was so much of my life that I had only superficially shared with her. That night I let it all out, everything.

I must have fallen asleep at some point because early the next morning my sister and Kim woke me up. They were sitting on the bed caressing my mom's head. Stroking her cheeks. Her breathing was erratic now. Excruciatingly long pauses between breaths. So long that we would gasp, thinking she had passed. Then another rattling breath would sneak up on us.

And then … there was no more. My mom had passed. The woman who had given me life left her own, lying in my arms.

We sat there silently … my sister, Kim, and I. A family bound in a moment of profound grief. Yet all of us in awe at the love and grace of the moment.

After awhile we called my Grandma June and a few close friends. Then the coroner came, zipped my mommy up in a plastic bag, and took her away.

A week later we held a memorial for her at her neighborhood church in Santa Clara, California. While my mom dealt with cancer, there had been such an outpouring of love and support for her that we knew there would be many people who wanted ... needed ... to say goodbye. And we were right.

The day of the memorial the church was full of people. Those who loved my mom filled the pews, the aisles, even the doorways. Everyone was dressed in tie-dye and Dallas Cowboy jerseys to honor my mom's passion for both.

My mom was a modest woman. No fame or fortune, her only treasure a heart that gave love to all who came into contact with her. There we were, looking out at hundreds of people—generations of kids who had stood in line to get her hugs, their parents, my mom's co-workers, friends, and everyday people who had experienced her love and were so moved that they felt called to share this moment.

We had planned a few speakers for the memorial. Each would be a representative of the different aspects of my mom's life. Kim talked about my mom as a wife. A woman named Cookie spoke about my mother's friendship. I shared my experience as her son. The parent of a now-grown child my mom had cared for spoke of her as a caregiver.

It was a moving service for the woman we all loved. Yet there were two speakers who truly defined my mom.

The first was her shoe guy. Yeah, imagine that. The guy who sold my mom shoes spoke at her memorial. I don't know about you but I don't have any idea who sold me my last pair of shoes. My mom did, though. You see, she had big feet, size 10 and double wide. She had struggled all her life to find shoes that would fit her properly. Later in life she would develop all kinds of foot issues, making it nearly impossible for her to find shoes. This man … the shoe guy … cared. He helped her, and so she went to him for years to buy shoes. In the process my mom touched his heart. The shoe guy spoke that day, representing the hundreds of random people whom my mom's love affected.

The second speaker was my daughter. My sister and I had asked the four grandkids—my children and hers—to participate in the memorial service. We asked that they pick one grandchild to speak. They chose Nataly. She would read the letter she had written her grandma before she died while the other three grandchildren stood with her as a sign of support for Nataly and love for their grandma.

Here is what my darling girl said that day:

Dear Grandma,

I've been wondering all day how I was going to start this. I don't know how I'm supposed to even cover everything in a page. It's all really too hard to talk about or even think about. Even though you know that I love you and how much you mean to me, I never really expressed to you the extent of it. And I really wish now that I had done this sooner because it doesn't seem right to me to always wait to do so 'til the very end.

I guess I'll start from the beginning. I don't remember our first meeting, but I always love hearing about it. How you thought I would never love you and how quickly that changed. And how I was your first grandchild and the first to call you grandma. I don't know if you ever knew how special that made me feel. I hear about how oftentimes adopted children may sometimes not feel completely part of the family, especially if they look so significantly different. I can honestly say that I have never had that problem. That has a lot to do with you because you never once made me feel like an adopted child or even made a mention of it. You have always been 105% my grandma. One of my favorite things about you is your way of making people feel so welcome and loved.

It's really hard not to be sad about this situation but what makes me feel better is all the memories I'm left with, because my happiest have been with you. To name a few: singing Baby Beluga on the way to Kinderwood, having discussions about "toe" trucks, blowing bubbles on your front porch, all those grandma shows, doing the duck-and-cover in your car and trying to look like a kidnapped hostage, all those delicious waffles you made me .... The truth is that the house you had next to Flower Jane's was my favorite place to be. Out of all the houses and apartments I've lived in, that house always felt most like home to me.

I don't know if you know this, but I have always been so grateful and so proud to have you as my grandma. You're truly the most caring, genuine, and loving person out there. I've always loved the fact that my grandma wasn't like everyone else's grandma. You weren't just some 70-year-old lady who wore too much perfume and played bingo. No, my grandma was younger than everyone else's grandma, had shorter hair than everyone else's grandma, danced better than everyone else's grandma, wore tie-dyed shirts, loved Harry Potter, never wore a bit of make-up, and had an amazing wife named Kim. You really are by far the coolest grandma a girl can ask for.

The fact that my time with you at this point is limited is too hard to come to grips with. But something that I've learned from you is to stay strong and stay positive. I'm just grateful for all of the memories I'm left with and for all of the things that you've done for me. Thank you for always wanting to listen when I needed someone to talk to, for helping me have such a happy childhood, for making me want to be a better person, and for giving me such an amazing dad (that wouldn't have been possible without you). I will always cherish the fact that I had such an incredible woman as my grandma. I love you so much and I always will.

Love, Nataly

It took time and distance for me to appreciate the gifts my mom had given me. Life, in the peculiar way it works, gave us a tragedy to bring us together and heal the wounds.

I am following my mother's path now. Her heart left me a breadcrumb trail that brought me here. In many ways it is her love that is writing this book ... still trying to give to the world.

·14·

ENRIQUE, THE HERO, AND A DIRT ROAD IN MEXICO

I WOKE UP EARLY. I GOT DRESSED IN MY CONCERT PROMOTER GARB —a T-shirt and jeans—and started on my way to the San Jose Arena, the new hockey arena home of the NHL Sharks.

This was my first big concert at Alvarez and Garner, the one I discussed earlier that turned our company around. Ruben and I had managed to score the biggest concert of the year, of the last several years perhaps.

Enrique Iglesias had burst onto the scene in 1995 with a Spanish album chock-full of hits. He followed it up in 1997 with *VIVIR* and the hits kept rolling. Now he was coming to San Jose, and I was the promoter.

I'd never promoted a big concert and I really had no idea what I was supposed to do that morning. But Ruben told me that one of us needed to be there, so, as the youngster, there I was.

It was 6:00 a.m. when I arrived and the production team was already hard at work building the stage and unloading trucks and crates. These are the behind-the-scenes heroes of the concert business, the men and women who put together the puzzle that ultimately helps the artist shine. (Behind-the-scenes heroes, for example, like Steve, who I would meet

127

much later in my career. He was a concert industry legend. Short and stocky with untamed red hair, he had been producing concerts for three decades. He was a storied veteran who, besides being the best at his trade, had a unique claim to fame. He had survived not one, not two, but three plane crashes with rock bands, including the well-known Lynyrd Skynyrd crash, and walked away with nothing but scarred memories and an almost myth-like status in the business.)

For the next eight hours I sat there watching the concert production assembled like a time-lapse picture, only this was in real time. Painstakingly slow.

Somewhere around 3:00 p.m. the intensity level of the venue rose and in walked the man of the hour, Enrique. Tall, lanky, and 22 years old at the time, he was three years younger than I was. I didn't know what to expect. I would soon find out.

He did a quick sound check, ran through versions of his hits, and then headed off the stage. I figured he would leave quickly, too busy to stick around. Instead he walked over to a pair of Hispanic women who were mopping a backstage floor. He said warmly, "Hi, I am Enrique." He shook their hands, then continued on until he had said hi to every employee on site. Eventually he ended up with me and we chatted for a minute.

I would go on to promote nearly 100 shows with Enrique over our careers. In many ways we grew up in the business together. I always admired his hard work and ability to maintain a child-like fun charisma.

Of course, in retrospect things are always funny, but at the time sometimes funny sucks.

Like the time we went to Las Vegas. On the plane ride home Enrique saw my new BlackBerry. He told me he was thinking of getting one and asked me if he could check it out. Of course I said yes and he spent the plane ride playing with it like an innocent child with a new toy ... or so I thought. When we landed, he gave it back to me with a twinkle in his eye.

On my drive home I began to receive strange messages from people in the industry. Things like "What?" ... "Are you OK?" ... and most disturbingly, "I never knew you felt that way ... ." Enrique had spent the entire flight sending love notes, sarcastic insults, and even a resignation letter to my boss. He then deleted the evidence and let me discover what he'd done, reply by excruciating reply from my surprised colleagues.

But the true story of Enrique, less fun but more telling as to his character, is this:

In the last months of my mom's life I took my entire family on a trip to Puerto Vallarta, Mexico. We rented a little house at the beach and enjoyed what would be our last vacation together. It was a welcomed reprieve from hospitals and doctors and therapies. Just a mom and her family, taking in the love.

Enrique was in town performing and so one night my sister and I went to see his show. He asked why I was in town and I told him. His face melted and he told me he wanted to come see my mom. I thanked him for that and figured it was one of those nice things people tell you and then never do.

Except the next day he texted me and asked for the address. He came later that day, but we were out at the beach and didn't hear the door. The next day I took my mom and family to swim with the dolphins at a nearby park. It was a stark realization of how sick my mom was as she was unable to get in the water with her favorite animals. She sat on the side of the pool, her feet dangling in the water, enjoying the sight of her children and grandkids playing with the beautiful dolphins.

As we were nearing the end of our adventure, Enrique texted me again that he was leaving town and wanted to stop by. I called and told him we were out. I thanked him for his kindness and told him it was okay, once again trying to let him off the hook, assuming it was just a hassle for him.

He stopped me and said clearly, "Jason, I want to do this. I'm going to head to the airport and let's meet in the middle so I can give your mom a hug."

And we did. We stopped at a gas station on a dirt road in Mexico where my mom and Enrique Iglesias chatted and laughed and hugged. It was a special moment for my mom, whose best understanding of what I did for work was always that I was Enrique Iglesias' promoter. And you know what? I was never prouder than that day to say this was true.

After my mom passed we encouraged friends and family to donate to the Lange Foundation in lieu of sending flowers. The program rescues animals set to be killed in Los Angeles-area shelters and gives them a second chance at life. In total we raised over $100,000, and guess who the biggest donor was?

We have a skewed definition of hero in our world. We judge heroism by money or fame or sports exploits when often the hero is a simple man or woman who touches the heart of another. A person who cares enough to make a difference.

Life is full of surprises, and sometime you discover a hero is a rock star on a dirt road in Mexico.

·15·

WATCHING DOLPHINS

ON NOVEMBER 3, 2010 *THE WALL STREET JOURNAL* RAN A STORY announcing my departure from Live Nation. It was a news story for about a day, then everyone went back to work. Life moved on, as it always does.

I learned a lesson when I was in grade school. My school held a fundraiser, you know the way schools do: whichever class sold the most would get an ice cream party. I was determined that my class would win, so I rallied the troops and pushed all my classmates to sell, sell, sell. We won.

On the day the party was scheduled, I woke up sick with a cold. My mom made me stay home. I was sure they would reschedule the ice cream party, positive that everyone would recognize my invaluable efforts and wait for me to return. Of course they didn't. The party went on and I'm sure everyone enjoyed their ice cream just fine without me.

I learned from the ice cream party that life goes on. Oh we can create drama and scandal and postpone the inevitable. But life always goes on.

So on November 3, 2010 I turned off my phone and my computer and went home.

The truth is there was no scandal. No drama to report. It was simply time. After a long and successful run, my career at Live Nation was over. I was exhausted. I'd lost my focus after my mom's passing. The deadlines and drama just didn't seem to matter as much any more. The truth is that not much in my life mattered at that point. Throw the horrible economy on top and it was a perfect storm. My division's numbers were down and I didn't have a solution. I was burned out and I needed to move on. Michael and I made a deal and, with tears in both our eyes, we hugged and I left.

I woke up the next day. For the first time in my life there was no answer to the question, "What do you do?" No longer was I the boy who worked to make his mommy proud ... she was gone. Nor was I the guy who ran the global concert division ... I was jobless. I opened my eyes and stared dead on into the question I had been working with Vera to answer: "Who am I?"

Only now there was no work to hide behind, no mask. Just me and nothing else.

For awhile I settled into thoughts of who I used to be. But that was depressing. Next I kept myself busy thinking of all that I *would* be. Dreaming about doing this. Planning to do that. The truth, though, is that I was tired, exhausted. Contemplating all I would do someday only made it worse.

I needed a simple answer, for myself and for the world. "What do I do?" I wanted an answer so opposite to anything I had ever said that it would shock me and everyone else into thinking a new way.

Then one day, sitting on the beach staring at the waves, my answer popped its head out of the water—"I watch dolphins." It was so perfect. Just what I was looking for. It would be my answer for the next two years.

You should have seen the expression on people's faces. Not sure if I was joking ... or crazy. In all honesty, I was a little of both. But it didn't matter. That silly little answer became my salvation as it forced me to find a new way to value myself.

Having created some breathing room for myself, I got back to the business of figuring out who I was. I decided to start at the beginning, to journey back through time. So I picked up the phone and started calling my mom's friends.

I gave them all the same background. Mom is gone and I'm on a journey to figure out who I am. I wanted—no insisted—on their help. I wanted to piece together the first few years of my life, and I needed their help to tell me everything that had gone on with my mom during that time. How she felt. What she did. How my dad treated her. What friends she had. Everything.

Here's what I found.

My mom became pregnant with me at age 20. She was so happy to be pregnant. She had always wanted to be a mom and now she was on her way. But she was also scared. All the fear and insecurity she had inherited from my grandma was bubbling out.

As a result, she did what we all do when we don't feel the way we think we're supposed to: she felt guilty. But my mom knew feeling guilty wasn't right either, so she layered on another level of guilt: feeling guilty for feeling guilty for being scared.

My dad was no help at all. He brought his own issues and dramas to the relationship, adding stress and anger to my mom's life. Apparently he yelled a lot. And broke things. My mom tried to keep the peace and held her feelings in.

There were also money issues. To be exact, there was no money. This worried my mom more. How would they pay the bills? What would happen after I was born? She started worrying that maybe having a baby wasn't the best idea.

While all this was going on, I was forming inside her. My brain, like that can of white paint I talked about in Chapter 13, slowly became tinted with the colors of the emotions my mom was feeling. Drop by drop I was learning what the world was like: scary and lonely. A world without money and support. A place where it wasn't okay to express your feelings. Instead you swallow them, keep the peace at all costs … and feel guilty.

UGGGHHH. Crazy right? All that going on and I wasn't even born yet.

So there I was interviewing my mom's friends, meeting with Vera, putting my life together bit by bit. Oh … and crying. In fact, I was getting so good at crying that once I even cried at an Adam Sandler movie!

I now had a pretty good understanding of my life in the womb. What my mom was up to. What feelings and beliefs she was feeling and transmitting to me. This had given me a good grip on my primary scenario and the early formation of my brain. Now I needed to get to know little me. What was I like as a child? What was going on in my world? Once again I turned to my mom's friends. They weren't sick of me yet so I kept on pumping them for information. Like a reporter desperate to get his scoop, I pushed and pried to get a glimpse of my early life.

They described me as "a little man in a boy's body." Always older than my age. Always helping my mom. Solving problems for myself. A perfect little child. Like an angel ... okay, okay, that's enough. But seriously, it was as though I had been born knowing my mom needed stability and maturity and that's what I provided.

Every once in awhile one of Mom's friends would get to talking and would give me a little too much information. I remember one conversation with ...well, I'll call her Martha to protect her reputation. I was talking to Martha and she was sharing this and that about my mom. She told me what a great friend my mom was. How they had shared secrets. Intimate secrets. Like the time Martha slept with two different men in the same week. AHHHHHHHH! EAR MUFFS, EAR MUFFS. WAY too much information!

I took that as I sign I had learned all I would from my mom's friends, so I started reading, just as I had all those years ago to learn business. I read

... and read ... and read. My ongoing mission was to further understand what made me tick.

In books like *A General Theory of Love*, *The Drama of the Gifted Child*, and *Biology of Belief* I found the answers I was looking for, rounding out what I was learning with Vera with additional nuggets that I applied in order to understand how I came to be.

While I was in the womb I'd learned about this scary place. My world. I'd learned about feeling alone and guilty. I'd learned that my dad couldn't be trusted, and that money was something that made my mommy feel scared inside. All of this mixed together in the paint can of my ever-expanding brain.

Then I was born. December 22, 1972. I and my already-tinted-paint-can brain popped into this world. I immediately began to observe the world and absorb everything. This is what we do for the first few years. Observe and absorb. It's how we learn so much so fast. Our brains are like a never-ending supply of Bounty paper towels picking up everything thrown our way.

We are driven by an untamed curiosity. We drink in the world exactly as we see it. The confusing part is that we aren't seeing it with fresh eyes. We're seeing it through the filter of all we learned in the womb. We are seeing the world from the same perspective as our moms because our paint is the same color.

The little Jason my mom's friends described to me wasn't a coincidence.

I was mature and helpful and good because all of my programming told me if I was good, I would be loved. I was forming exactly as I had been taught to get the affection all little children desire.

The final piece is DNA. Carried forward in all human DNA, mine and yours, is a strong will to survive. That's good right? Well, yes. But it also comes with an interesting twist.

What exactly does survive mean? What was my DNA telling me I needed to do to survive? It was telling me to make the right decision. Why? Because historically a wrong decision meant I would end up being eaten by a saber-toothed tiger, or freezing in the snow, or eating a poisonous berry. So to keep myself safe ... to keep all of us safe ... my DNA was instructing my brain to see the world in a way that made it right. "But what is right?" The only version of right we know is the "right" of the tinted paint in our paint can. It's the story of the world taught to us subconsciously by our parents, in my case the family story passed down from Grandma June, to my mom, and now to me.

Do you see where this is all going?

The little me, Toddler Jason, was armed with a brain that believed the world was scary and lonely. That daddy was mean. That money caused pain. That I was all alone. PLUS genetic programming that required my brain to be right, to make those beliefs a reality.

So who was I destined to become? What was my life story guaranteed to be unless I made some dramatic changes? Exactly what it was for my grandma. Identical to the world of my mom. And exactly what I had been living for the first 37 years of my life. Scared. Alone. Never feeling good enough.

If you need any more evidence of the strength of this family programming, consider this. When my grandma's mom died and her dad left them to sit on that bar stool, she was left alone to take care of her two brothers. Years later my mom would be divorced and left alone to raise her two children. My uncle (my mom's brother) would die in a motorcycle accident, leaving his wife alone with two children. I would later be divorced and left alone with two children. And my sister? You guessed it: divorced and alone with two children.

HOLY SHIT.

I didn't know whether to cry, barf, or jump for joy at what I was learning.

Yeah Jason, but you made a lot of money. That was different, wasn't it? It was different in that I made more money than my mom. Still, our perception of money was the same. She didn't have it and was scared. I had it and was scared. She always felt she needed more. So did I. We were just living two different sides of the same coin. In all the important, internal ways, I was just like my mother.

I had my DNA telling me to be right, my family story screaming inside telling me to work hard and that I wasn't good enough. While everyone saw a superstar when they looked at me, inside I was a ticking time bomb. Just like my mom, I was trapped in a vicious cycle. Overworked, feeling under-appreciated, resentful, yet all the while secretly craving the dysfunction that was pulsing inside me. So I created it over and over again. Relationship after relationship. Job after job. Futile conversation after futile conversation with the voices in my head.

I had to stop this.

* * *

It was July 18, two years to the day after the passing of my mom. I was living on the beach in a small community south of the Los Angeles airport.

My daily practice was to walk on the beach. I would get going, soaking up the Southern California sun, and sometimes walk for hours. Some days it was meditative with my mind a gentle calm; on other days my brain whirled like a hamster on a wheel.

Today I was melancholy, which is hard to explain to those who haven't lost their parents. Psychologists have a name for it (of course they do). They call it "Adult Orphan Syndrome," and given what I knew about my family history, this label made sense to me.

Like most labels, this one also tells a story of its own. It diagnoses the feeling but also carries with it the baggage of what that label means in the world. The way grape juice quenches your thirst but leaves your teeth purple, so it was for me. My sadness became loneliness and then, as I settled into being an adult orphan, abandonment.

As I walked I looked at my feet. Head down, feeling really sorry for myself. Remembering my mom. Missing her hugs. Reflecting on the awful disease that took her. Her strained last breaths. The horrible rattling in her chest. Lying on the bed holding her lifeless body. Then the tears started to flow. Really flow.

I was sobbing when I became distracted by my feet. Step after step, I looked down at the footprints, like a trail of sad memories as I walked along.

I remembered that poem, "Footprints in the Sand," by Mary Stevenson. You know the one. A person has a dream of reviewing their life with God. They look at their journey and see there were often two sets of footprints, their own and those of God, who had been walking alongside them. But in the really tough moments, there was only one set of footprints. God is asked why he would leave them all alone in their times of greatest need.

God replies, "The times when you have seen only one set of footprints is when I carried you."

My mom loved that poem. It was a fixture in our home, traveling with us from the old pink trailer in Arizona to our many apartments and homes in California. From relationship to relationship and job to job, "Footprints" was always there. At times it was a cut-out paper version, others a wood carving. There was even a laminated hand-written one my sister or I had given my mom.

Thinking of the poem, remembering my mom, I plodded along all by myself, an empty beach and an empty man.

Then I had a calling. Not a voice, but a "knowing" that I should look to the sea. So I did.

There, swimming in perfect rhythm with my steps, was a lone dolphin, gently gracing the water, dipping in and out of the waves as dolphins do.

Dolphins were my mom's favorite animal; she had them everywhere. Dolphin calendars, dolphin souvenirs given to her by the children she looked after. A dolphin was the gift guaranteed to bring a smile to my mom's face. Dolphins filled her home.

I walked for a mile with that dolphin. It never sped up or changed direction, nor did I. We just meandered along, the dolphin, my mom, and I.

Then it hit me, and I smiled the warm smile of a comforted child. I wasn't alone. I just needed to look up from my walk and notice who was with me.

·*16*·

GREEN JUICE, HAPPY CELLS, AND A MAN CALLED AVOCADO

WHEN I FIRST MOVED TO LOS ANGELES, A FRIEND OF MINE AT THE OFFICE looked at me and asked, "Do you work out?" This was not a compliment. He wasn't admiring my six-pack abs. I replied simply, "No," to which he replied, "YET."

You see, as I would soon learn, everyone in LA works out, is on some diet or another, or has plastic surgery. In this way, everything you have ever seen or read or thought about LA is absolutely true.

Just as my friend predicted, I began to work out. I got a membership at Sports Club/LA, a place so cool they had to put the LA at the end so you would realize how cool it was. I pretty much worked out non-stop from that point on, sometimes more, sometimes less.

My eating was another story. I was in LA, the city of business lunches and dinners and star-studded cocktail parties. So what did I do? I ate a lot, and drank too much, and had a ton of fun. I partied like a rock star just as you would expect.

My thoughts on health began to change while my mom was dying of cancer. My daughter, Nataly, had begun to follow a vegetarian diet and believed her new understanding could help my mom. One day at my house in Los Angeles my mom, children, sister, and nephews were in my living room watching some stupid comedy. Nataly paused the movie and asked her grandma, my mom, if she would watch a documentary called *A Beautiful Truth* (not to be confused with Al Gore's *An Inconvenient Truth*). *A Beautiful Truth* is about saving our bodies, specifically, the Gerson Therapy for preventing and curing cancer with green fruit and vegetable juice. Nataly was so sincere. Her eyes welled with tears as she pleaded with my mom to watch it with her. They didn't watch the movie because I think my mom had surrendered to the cancer at that point. She was intent on living the last weeks of her life loving her family, not fighting a disease. Nataly's documentary, and the lessons she was learning on her own, would return to play a huge role in our family.

Some months later, my girlfriend at the time asked me if I would join her on the Daniel Fast, a fast based on what Daniel did in the Bible. I laughed and said, "I've tried lots of things in my life, how bad can a fast be?"

I committed myself to a three-day fast, Friday, Saturday, and Sunday—only fresh fruit, vegetables, and whole grains. No sweeteners, no meat, no chicken or eggs, no caffeine, no processed flour or artificial anything, and no alcohol.

When you press the pause button on your diet this dramatically, you get some major eye-openers. For me the first was how dependent I was on food. How my entire day was planned around breakfast, lunch, and dinner. How I instinctively HAD to eat at certain times, even when I paid attention and wasn't hungry. It was a habit.

The next big lesson for me was that I was addicted to caffeine. I had only been addicted to one other substance in my life and that's how I knew the symptoms of withdrawal. After my first divorce, when I was raising the kids and running my business, I began to have panic attacks. I'll never forget the first time. I was driving from a meeting to school to pick up Nataly. My mind was racing through all the things I had to do; I was cursing the slow traffic and dreading the look on my little girl's face, picturing her sitting on the curb, all alone, waiting for me. Then it hit. A hot flash like sticking your head in an oven … my heart pounding like it was burrowing free from my chest … the road in front of me blurry … and I thought, "Oh my God, I'm going to die!"

But I wasn't. I would find out later from a psychiatrist that it was a panic attack, a reaction to all the stress I was under. He prescribed Xanax and told me to take it until the stress went away. And that was the problem, because as we've all learned, the stress never goes away. So I kept taking the Xanax, for two years, every day, until a friend filled me in on the health risks. I quit, cold turkey.

That's when the withdrawal symptoms started. Severe muscle cramps, ringing in the ears, blurry vision, headaches, a desire to jump out the window. Funny how the remedy gives you the same symptoms as the ones you're treating.

But back to the caffeine: when I went on the fast, all the same symptoms started happening again and I realized I was experiencing caffeine withdrawal. I didn't drink THAT much coffee ... did I? I only went to Starbucks in the morning after dropping Kevin at school: one. After lunch or while on a walk: two. Sometimes, most times, after dinner: three. Then there were the cappuccino-flavored muscle milks: four, five, six. And the other miscellaneous places caffeine sneaks into a diet. In all, I was consuming the equivalent of six to eight cups of coffee a day! Now I was paying the price.

I wasn't just addicted to caffeine. My favorite restaurant was a vegetarian's nightmare, Fogo de Chao, a smorgasbord of meat the waiters bring to you in a continuous flow of different cuts so you don't even have to get out of your chair. You just gorge yourself on meat and red wine until you, somehow, hobble out of the place after enjoying a dessert to top it all off.

By Sunday night the withdrawal had subsided. The fast was over. After all that pain, however, I wasn't about to go back to my old habits, so I stuck with the fast as I learned more about my health.

One day in the early days of this experience, Nataly came over and brought her health movies ... *Fat, Sick and Nearly Dead, Forks Over Knives,* and *A Beautiful Truth.* They opened my eyes to a whole new idea about diet. The concept that we eat to give our body the fuel it needs to function, not to satisfy our habits. The movies teach that our bodies are natural healing machines and if we fuel them with nutrient-dense foods, we can take huge steps toward eliminating the diseases that plague our bodies.

The movies introduced me to juicing, making homemade fresh juices from fruits and vegetables. Scary for some but a welcome idea for me. You see, I had never liked eating salad, or rabbit food as I called it. The beauty of juicing was that I could consume an entire salad, actually three or four, in one juice.

I went out and bought a juicer, some apples, kale, chard, and romaine lettuce. I went home and tried it out. One apple, a bunch of kale—wow, I saw what they were talking about as it took a ton of kale to produce even a little juice! Then I juiced the chard and some romaine and there it was... my very first green juice. A very very green green juice. Okay. Here I go. I'm going to drink it now. Oh shit, it smells like a freshly-mowed lawn on a Sunday afternoon. Okay, I can do this. No problem. Can't be worse than a Jägermeister shot. AWWWWWW! Yes it was.

Turns out one apple isn't enough on your first try.

I added more apple and a lemon, which sweetened the drink and smoothed out the flavors. Then I enjoyed my first juice. It was actually good. More importantly, the next day I felt a little spring in my step. So I kept juicing. And I kept feeling better and better. My skin was glowing, I slept better, I had a sustained all-day energy unlike the highs and crashes from caffeine.

Before long all I was doing was juicing. I woke up in the morning and made juice for my son Kevin (note: show the movies mentioned above to your kids, they're much smarter than we give them credit for and are more easily adaptable because of their age) and made two or three for myself. Then I would repeat the process in the evening. I felt amazing, but after a few months I was beginning to look like I had just come out of a long journey through the desert. Too skinny.

What to do now?

Go to the grocery store of course. Maybe I was being too extreme. There must be some easy meals I can buy at the grocery store without artificial or processed ingredients, right?

This was another eye-opening experience. How could it be that nearly everything in a standard grocery store is made from non-whole foods and processed ingredients? Item by item, shelf by shelf, I hunted for things that would comply with my new-found diet. Strike out. Next I went to Whole Foods and there I found a much more friendly world. The employees knew what I was talking about. I still had to search, and many items still contained artificial ingredients, but I was able to find the snacks and variety I was looking for.

While the green juice was quenching my body's thirst for nutrients, my mind was thirsty for information. I watched the documentaries over and over. I read every book and blog on vegetarian lifestyle I could find, which is where I found out about David Wolfe. "Avocado" as he is affectionately called.

David, from all my reading, appeared to be the expert on the raw food diet—eating and juicing raw fruits, vegetables, grains, and the superfoods and herbs I would learn about next.

I found out that David was speaking at a health conference, "Longevity Now," near me. I tracked down his assistant, who it turned out (thank you, Universe) had worked at Live Nation and knew who I was. She helped me set up a consultation with David.

Nataly and I drove down to the Orange County Hilton to meet David Wolfe, who is a bit like the Tasmanian Devil, a whole ton of energy packed into a small body. He greeted us warmly. Wearing his signature poncho and sporting long, curly hair like a Rasta man, he asked us to sit down.

I gave him a quick rundown of what I'd been doing. The fast. The juicing. How good I felt. My concerns about withering away. He laughed a familiar laugh that said he understood.

Then he gave us a two-hour class that changed my life. For those of you who are familiar with David, you will totally understand when I say there is no humanly possible way to summarize all that David taught us that day. He is like an encyclopedia mixed with a pinball machine, pinging unpredictably from one informative data point to the next. He is an amazing resource, but I wouldn't want to be the one who has to transcribe it all!

Here are the four biggest take-aways that helped me ... and I think can help you:

1.   Foods you like are a delivery vehicle for the nutrients you need. Come again? Okay, what do you like? For me, the answer was banana smoothies (banana, fresh coconut water, and ice). Whatever the answer—orange juice, strawberries, chocolate, almond milk, etc.—once you find a flavor you love, it is now your decoy delivery vehicle. Now your job is to pack it full of every nutrient you can. Just like a FedEx truck doesn't go out with just one package, you want to pack your delivery vehicle sky-high with as many things as possible to supercharge your body.

2.   What foods pack the most punch? This is where superfoods come in. What are superfoods? For a complete list buy David's book of the same name, but here is a brief description. Superfoods are like the power pellets in the video game Pac-Man. They are extremely nutrient-dense foods from around the world that contain high levels of vitamins, minerals, enzymes, and compounds that are difficult to get in our busy lives. Superfoods boost energy, keep the immune system strong and healthy, enhance circulation (note to men: "enhanced circulation" to all areas of your body = no need for little blue pills!), and help you feel young and vital. Some common superfoods are things like cacao (natural chocolate, a high source of protein and magnesiuim); spirulina (protein); hemp (protein and essential fatty acids); maca (energy and hormone balance); acai (antioxidant and immune booster); and goji berry (longevity and brain enhancement),

to name a few. Using these superfoods we take an ordinary banana smoothie and transform it into a SuperMan Elixir. Starting my day with a smoothie is one of the most impactful and easiest changes that I first made and follow to this day.

3.   Listen to your body. Everyone is different and our constitutions are all unique, so listen to everyone's advice as a guideline and then see what works for you. As you begin to clear out the sugars and caffeine from your body you quiet down. When your body is quiet you can hear your cells. They will tell you what brings them joy and what doesn't. Just keep experimenting until you find what your community of cells likes.

4.   Chinese herbs. Chinese herbs I asked? What's that? David's answer was, "go see Ron Teeguarden." I would, and that's another essay later on.

Armed with this new information, I set off to build upon my new foundation of health. Using the juices and smoothies as a base, I experimented with the rainbow of superfoods that can be found at Whole Foods or online. These new concoctions made me feel stronger, more vibrant, and added to the joy I was already feeling.

I know at this point what many of you may be thinking: "Great Jason, but it's really hard to stop eating foods I like. I know they aren't fueling my body but I just can't stop eating them."

That's true. It's hard. Really hard, because we've formed habits like I had with caffeine and Xanax. It's a vicious cycle fueled by the very foods and drinks we consume. I used to go to the coffee shop, buy a latte, then see the pastries and buy a chocolate chip muffin. With my body racing from the sugar and caffeine, not operating from my core, I spent the rest of my day in a spin. The cycle goes on and on from there.

Then the guilt would kick in, because I knew I wasn't supposed to eat the sugar and drink the caffeine, so on top of the substances I'd put into my body I layered on the guilt. I felt badly about this or that. I felt I wasn't good because I ate whatever. So let me share the number one thing I have learned about our bodies. I'll write it in bold and all caps to be very dramatic, because it's that important:

GUILT AND STRESS ARE WORSE FOR YOUR BODY THAN ANYTHING YOU EAT ... PERIOD.

To understand this I had to learn to look at my body in a different way than I was used to. I found a new perspective based on the science of my friend and teacher, Dr. Bruce Lipton. Bruce is an amazing man. He spent most of his life as a cellular biologist, a serious, world-renowned scientist. He studied cells in a petri dish for a living. Not exactly a fun-sounding guy, but he is. Bruce has taken all that heady learning and applied it to how our bodies work. He does it in an affable and every-guy kind of way. His books are a must-read, especially *Biology of Belief.*

Bruce teaches that our body is really a community of cells. In fact, approximately 50 trillion cells. Fifty trillion! Each of these cells is a mini-you. Each of them carries your DNA and feels your stress, your joy, your love, your pain. And they each have a job. They work in groups just like we do at work. They get together and make an eye, or a lung, or your heart, or your brain, in what amounts to a bunch of tiny cells working together to make you tick.

I learned from Bruce that there is something else very important about these cells—they are always doing one of two things. They're either sensing joy, staying fluid and flexible and receiving nutrients and excreting waste; or they sense fear and constrict, locking out nutrients and trapping in toxins.

Joyful cells = healthy cells

Scared cells = sick cells

Because the health of your body is a direct reflection of the health of your cells, you can see how important it is to avoid stress and guilt and experience as much joy as possible.

For all the men who just said, "Huh?" let me give you an example that helped me understand. When our cells are experiencing joy (think 50 trillion cells at a strip club), they're open and strong and growing. When they experience cellular fear (like your wife finding out you went to that strip club), they shut down, they atrophy, and they experience dis-ease, or disease ... like cancer, diabetes, obesity, etc.

If my strip club analogy made any sense to you (and if you say it didn't you're lying), then you can see that experiencing stress or guilt around your diet is 100% counterproductive as it raises the fear level of your cells and will cause you to get sick.

To get out of the vicious cycle the first thing I learned to do was to stop the guilt. In fact, a wise teacher of mine taught me an exercise I want to share with you so, together, right now, we can actually have an experience of health without guilt.

Let's take a really deep breath together: in through the nose and out through the mouth—a really deep inhale through your nostrils and then exhale freely from your mouth. Do this five or six times until you feel the tension in your body reduced and your mind a little quieter.

Now let's close our eyes. Oh shit, that doesn't work while you're reading! Okay then, keep your eyes open and let's take a moment to honor our bodies. What does that mean? Let's just put aside, for a moment, the changes we want to make and the parts of our body we want to improve and just sit and imagine, with gratitude, the journey on which our bodies, the 50 trillion cells, have taken us. The journey from a small spark of spirit to these amazing beings we are today. Through childhood ... all the scraped knees and bumps and bruises. Your first kiss. The ups and downs of love that followed. Your body has been there. Loyally, faithfully holding you up. Thank it. I know this is odd, I thought so too the first time I did it, but go with me for a moment. You know I'm not cuckoo so let's trust together in this experience and honor the challenges our bodies have taken us through—any disease, pain, surgery, struggles. Our bodies held strong and got us here. The fact that we're here means everything has worked out okay. Everything is just fine. Because we are all here together.

Take a few more deep breaths and let it sink in, this amazing feeling of love and gratitude for your body.

From this place of gratitude I have learned there is only one way out of a vicious cycle, and that's to create a benevolent one. A benevolent cycle is one that is friendly to our body, one that fills us with nutrients, love, and healthy joy. This is no harder than creating the initial unhealthy habit. We think it is because we're hooked, but once we kick the old habit, forming the new, positive one is no harder. Think about it for a moment.

It wasn't easy to fill my body with substances that I knew for a fact would slow me down, harm my brain, and quite possibly give me a self-inflicted feeling of a really bad case of the flu. It was just a habit.

It wasn't easy to drink a cup of liquid that accelerated my heart, raised my adrenaline, spiked my cortisol, and then made me crash and burn a few hours later. It was just a habit.

It wasn't easy to eat an animal filled with hormones and raised in an unsanitary environment; an animal that moments before being slaughtered released death hormones to every part of its body and was later butchered, frozen, and hauled across the country, only to be fried and served up as a burger that could clog my arteries, lead to cardiac arrest, raise my chance of diabetes, and cause a host of other illnesses. It was just a habit.

And it wasn't easy to consume a beverage in a shiny can or a snack in a foil wrapper that was loaded with the equivalent of 30 packs of sweetener, a beverage or a snack with a high probability of leading to diabetes and obesity … it, too, was just a habit.

The good news is that I learned achieving good health is no harder than what I was already doing. It's the same habit, just a different road. The fact that I did, in the past, have a habit that was unhealthy is no different from driving somewhere and turning down the wrong street.

So when I found myself in a vicious cycle, I simply learned to:

1. STOP

2. TURN AROUND

3. GO THE RIGHT WAY

The remedy for a wrong turn in health is exactly the same as getting lost while driving:

1. STOP one negative habit

2. TURN IT AROUND by replacing it with a positive

3. GO THE RIGHT WAY by doing one more positive

It's that simple. A habit is just three steps in one direction—negative or positive. We don't have to make this into a bigger deal or, worse, make ourselves wrong. We don't have to beat ourselves up or guilt-trip ourselves until our cells scream out by expressing disease. I learned to keep it simple and light and easy:

1. skip the morning caffeine

2.   have a fresh green juice instead

3.   enjoy a healthy lunch

Then give yourself a big hug. You did it!

You've learned by now that I tend to jump right in, go all out. If that isn't how you do things, don't. There is no magic formula. The only thing that matters is that you just take steps, one by one, day by day. If you find yourself going the wrong way, just stop, turn around, and go the other way. Always giving yourself a hug. Always honoring your body for the effort.

Remember that you are the president of the cellular community called your body. The whole purpose is to bring joy to our cells. Just like a presidential election is won state by state, your cellular election is won step by step, meal by meal, and day by day.

Altering what I put in my body was the first step in re-tinting the paint of my life. Replacing old habits, learned over a lifetime, with new, healthier ones that reflected who I wanted to be. Changing my diet would be the first drops of white in that murky paint I had inherited. Soon I would be adding many, many more.

·17·

THE PRESIDENT, THE PASTOR, AND A GAY MARRIAGE MADE IN HEAVEN

A FEW DAYS BEFORE PRESIDENT OBAMA ARRIVED IN LOS ANGELES FOR the largest fundraiser in the history of presidential politics (the event at George Clooney's house I mentioned in the intro to this book), he made an announcement. Perhaps he did it because he needed an issue to rally Hollywood after angering the entertainment community with his position against tougher piracy law, or maybe it was just time to do the right thing. The reason is not important; what is important is that President Obama came out in support of gay marriage.

This simple declaration of human rights by the President of the United States set off a firestorm within the Christian community, especially because the president had cited his Christian faith as the basis for his decision.

Since my departure from Live Nation, I had been attending a small Christian church in my neighborhood. A new spirituality was awakening in me. I was longing for a sense of community and support, and while I had never been a regular church-goer as an adult, I found something I was thirsting for—the songs, the hugs, and most of all, the beautiful teachings of Jesus.

"Love thy neighbor as thyself … faith can move mountains … God loves everyone … ask and you shall receive … ."

Like many things in my adult life, gay marriage was an issue highlighted for me by my mother.

* * *

One day in 2000 my mom asked me to stop by her house in the Burbank area of San Jose. She lived in a small, two-bedroom cottage with a garden of sunflowers she had planted herself. It wasn't much of a house, but to my mom it was her little slice of heaven. In her typical giving fashion, she had searched high and low to find a place where her aging mom could live close by. And so it was that my Grandma June lived in the cottage next to my mom's.

My mom had a concerned look on her face that day, which wasn't surprising because she was always worried about something. Usually it was about someone else—a stray dog, a child at school, a sick friend—but today it was about her, or me … well, you'll understand in a minute.

She asked me to sit down and then her eyes teared up. She told me she loved me and never wanted to disappoint me. Where was this going? I wondered.

Then she told me that she was in love with a woman—her friend Kim to be precise.

I chuckled inside as this neither surprised nor concerned me. My mom's love life had always been unique and I really liked Kim. With a smile I said, "Mom, I love you and the truth is I like Kim a lot better than all the asshole men you've dated." And that was that.

My mom and Kim dated for several years. Mom was happier than I'd ever seen her before. She'd found love, finally, after all those years of searching.

Eight years later my mom married Kim in a ceremony on the beach in Monterey, California. This was in the brief period when gay marriage was legal, before the passage of Proposition 8. It was a raucous time: gay couples rushed to express their love and commitment while opponents protested and politicked for a constitutional ban.

For many in California, and around the country, this was a news story. For my family it was personal as hate reared its horned head in our face.

Kevin, Nataly, and I drove up from Los Angeles for the wedding. We arrived in Monterey late and spent the night at the Hilton Hotel. The next morning we got dressed for the ceremony. On strict instructions from the bride and bride, it was a casual event: jeans and tie-dye and tennis shoes comprised the dress code.

As we neared the site where many gay weddings were going on that day, we noticed a commotion ahead. There were a dozen or so people, holding signs and yelling at cars. Their message was expressed with slogans like:

"God hates fags."

"Jesus loves you and has a wonderful plan for your life in HELL."

"Homosexual marriage is terrorism."

And ... "God created Adam and Eve, not Adam and Steve."

Nataly, a teenager then and in that great time of life when you have no patience for stupidity, rolled down the window and expressed what the entire family (and much of the world) was feeling.

"FUCK YOU!" she yelled.

That same year Live Nation was one of the first companies in California to publicly and financially support opposition to Prop 8.

Five years later politicians finally decided to endorse gay marriage, a welcome though overdue turn of events for me. With or without their support, my mom and thousands of others were already in loving relationships and the tide of support for gay marriage was well underway.

What set me on my heels was the reaction of my Christian friends. This was a serious issue for them. In their minds gay marriage broke God's law. Through them I became acquainted with the less loving portions of the Bible. Like Jude 1:7, where God punishes homosexuals in eternal fire. Leviticus 18:22, which calls homosexuality an abomination. And Leviticus 20:13, which prescribes the death penalty for gays.

This was a strong departure from the loving message of Jesus, an about-face from the songs of community and support, a new face of a church I had come to trust as my friends.

So I called my friend Pastor Paul.

I met Paul for the first time one day after a pre-Christmas service at the church. He had delivered a passionate, loving, and tender call of support for all the people in our community who were suffering during the holidays. He so moved me that I dropped the 500 or so dollars I had in my pocket in the collection basket. I followed up with a call to the church on Monday to see how else I could help.

Paul had a long list of people who were in need: a single mom of four children who had lost her job, a father who had been injured at work and had no money for his family, an elderly grandma without food, and on and on. Together Paul and I would help them all and many, many others over the next year as we bonded through acts of kindness. This was exactly the kind of loving service I had been looking for.

As the gay marriage debate raged on, I drove over to meet with Paul and get this cleared up. I started with a simple question.

"Pastor Paul, if Jesus says love your neighbor as yourself, how can the church oppose people who love each other?"

Paul squirmed as if sensing this was going to be one of "those" conversations. He replied by telling me that Christians love everyone and want to help them. That we all sin, and so homosexuals are just like others who needed to find the light.

Hmm. I didn't consider my mom a sinner nor someone who needed to find the light. Ok, so let's make this more personal.

"Pastor Paul, is my mom in hell because she loved Kim?"

"We don't know that," he explained, "because she may have repented."

Repented? For loving? You think my mom, the woman who made feisty, stubborn me, repented for loving another human being?

Okay, now it was time to be more direct. "Assuming my mom didn't repent, is she in heaven or hell?"

"Well, the Bible IS the word of God, and so, well…" I could see the pain in my friend's face. He so wanted to give me the logical, loving answer. He wanted to tell me my mom was an angel. But he couldn't. He looked down before finishing, "she would not be in heaven."

I know this answer wouldn't come as surprise to some people. Those who have suffered bigotry in their lives have come to expect this kind of duality. "I'm loving, but not toward THEM." Still, I was floored. This was my friend, my pastor … how could he believe my mom deserved to be in hell?

"Paul, are you saying that if someone doesn't believe and act exactly as you say they should, they will burn in hell?"

"Not the way I say, Jason," he said quickly. "Act the way God says they should."

"But my mom spent her entire life helping, giving, caring. There was no person more Christ-like than my mother. And because of whom she chose to love … God says she's going to hell?!"

I realized this was getting too personal and too heated, so I changed veins to an example with a little less charge.

"Paul, let's say there's a little girl who lives in the mountains of ... China. She lives with her mom and dad and there's no one else around. Their entire life is spent walking the forest, communing with nature, and loving all they see. As her parents grow old she cares for them, cooking and bathing and tending to their every need. After they die she continues to live alone, just this beautiful soul and nature. Now she never sees a Bible and never knows of Jesus. In every way she exemplifies a Christ-like life, but has not accepted Jesus as her Lord and Savior. Where does she go when she dies?"

Once again Paul was pained. He tried to answer "We don't know," but I pressed. I was now filled with the sting of injustice and I wasn't going to let him off.

"Paul," I said, "is the little girl going to burn?"

The answer was yes.

I was deeply saddened. I so wanted Paul to have a different answer, one that would bridge the gap between the Old Testament and the world in which I lived today ... the world in which my mom's life and death had taken a public policy issue and made it real.

Paul was—is—a good man. A caring man who spends his nights comforting the homeless, a kind soul who runs the youth camp in the summer, a hero to those in pain who need some love. But because he believes all that good comes from the words in a book, he is also a bigot trapped by his own religion into believing that love is only love when the book says it is. And hate is only hate when it's not his people doing the hating.

Before I left, Paul looked at me longingly and said, "Jason, you are such a good Christian man.... ." He didn't finish his sentence, and I didn't reply. There was nothing left to say.

I had spent my entire life writing my own story. A lifetime of not really fitting into any box. I guess it shouldn't have been a surprise to me that religion would be no different.

I was looking for a story to understand God, not one written in stone, but told from the heart. One that made as much sense today as it did a thousand years ago and as it would in another thousand years. I would find what I was looking for in due time.

For now I had learned another life lesson, again with the help of my mom: to always follow my heart no matter what the book says.

·18·

MY MEDITATION, MEETING THE GURU

I ARRIVED EARLY. I'M NEVER EARLY, ANYWHERE. BUT I DIDN'T WANT TO be late today. Surely that's not a good first impression when meeting a guru. Little did I know one of this guru's many slogans was designed to explain his perpetual tardiness: "You can't rush spirituality."

I opened the side gate as I had been instructed in the voice mail message. I walked into a yard. More like a secret garden. Plants, trees, green everywhere. And statues ... frogs ... happy Buddha ... lots of frogs.

A kind woman dressed in all white greeted me. She walked me through the gentle jungle-like yard to a standalone room at the back of the property. Then she said calmly, "He will be with you soon."

I didn't know what to expect. I had seen pictures of Guru Singh on the Internet. Tall, alabaster skin and hair. Piercing blue eyes. Long white beard. A bright orange turban topping a costume of white robes. Like a thinner Dumbledore mixed with the magic carpet-riding swamis I had seen on TV in the Sunday morning cartoons from my youth.

Now here I was, waiting to meet him. My heart skipped joyfully, like a kid in the schoolyard. I learned long ago such situations always turned into one of two things: a great new adventure or one hell of a story. Sometimes both.

I glanced around the room, neatly cluttered with a million and one trinkets, statues, stones, and pictures. There was a large mirror to my right covered with saying after saying, as if a child had gotten carried away with a label maker. Things like "Are you in a relation-SHIP or a relation-canoe? Can you stand up?" And "Be flexible. Water is so flexible we call it solution."

To my left was a table covered in little frogs. "What is it with frogs?" I thought. A meditating frog, a green jade frog, a wooden one, frog after frog.

When I was little my grandma loved elephants. On every birthday, every Christmas and every Mother's Day we gave her an elephant. Until one day she told us directly, "No more damn elephants." This guy clearly had not done the same. I had never seen this many frogs.

Then he walked in, interrupting my analysis of the surroundings. "Sat Nam," he said. He looked into my eyes. Holding his gaze. He looked at me. I looked back at him. Not like a stare, it wasn't threatening. More like a warm hug drawing me in, followed by something deeper. I couldn't look away. His eyes and mine, in sync, like two computers, recognizing, remembering. A silent download of years of information from his soul to mine.

Then he smiled a giant, "Where ya been all these years?" kind of smile.

As if he had been waiting for me.

I was home.

There I sat. A stranger in a strange land, yet knowing deeply I had been here before; maybe many times.

When he spoke it was as though he already knew why I was there, not needing any questions or prompting.

"We arrive at every location in our life, every moment in our life, through a series of micro-decisions and micro-moments. This is actually established by a greater equation that has been guiding us through thousands upon thousands upon thousands of lifetimes, an equation known as destiny.

"You, in fact, have arrived in this room through such a series of events. All the sensations you are experiencing at this very moment: the curiosity, the partial concern, the overriding joy, and the accompanying reasons that you claim brought you here—are all careening together to express this moment, as this moment.

"Everyone will eventually wind up in this room. It may be a room on a different planet. It may be a room on a different continent. It may be a room in a different country. Regardless of where and when, everyone will eventually wind up in this room asking the questions that brought you here today."

I sat there wide-eyed, mesmerized by his words. There was nothing to say, so I listened quietly to my new teacher.

"The journey to this room takes a very long time, but from the perspective of where the journey has originated or is being managed it takes no time at all. The management of this journey is what many have speculated to be God. But God, in that context, is an invention of the mind and for that reason they have developed many different belief systems. One of the most certain facts is that we were developed very intelligently, not haphazardly, and therefore to follow that development has meaning. How does a person arrive at this room with the questions that look beyond earning to survive and then earning to be the wealthiest person around and then earning beyond that just for the sake of earning? That's the answer that you are obviously looking for and it's the same kind of answer that a child is looking for when it's lying on its belly able to move but unable to travel. Before that child learns to crawl it observes all of those moving about it. Before an adult child reaches beyond, they get a good job, get a good car, get a good house, get a good life, and reach into the realms beyond, it sits just like that child in a complete state of frustration."

"Is he reading my mind?" I thought. I didn't know how, but he seemed to sense what was going on in my head.

"Envy mixed with frustration mixed with anger mixed with compromise mixed with jealousy mixed with observation mixed with determination. All of these developmental sensations come crashing together in order to break the human from its shell. The shell of that mega-story that life is a challenge, perhaps a struggle, striving to be on top and then you die. And that's why you're here in this room, like that little baby on its stomach."

Then he said, "So … tell me the story of Jason, what makes you tick?"

I told him my story. Growing up poor. Working my whole life. Selling gum. The flea market. Chávez. Spanish concerts. Clear Channel. Live Nation. My mom's death. Watching dolphins. Vera. The books I'd read. "I'm here," I said, "because I want to know God. I hope you can help me."

He smiled, straightened his spine. He asked me to cross my legs.

We meditated. I had never meditated before. Well, once I had tried it after reading a Deepak Chopra book. Tried it. But that was it.

I sat there with my eyes closed, my mind racing. A few seconds passed—a few seconds that felt like an hour. He spoke soothingly, "Just let the thoughts come. Don't resist. They are like radio waves. You can't stop them. Just let them come and go. Don't engage."

But I did engage. Of course I did. We all do in the beginning. It was impossible to quiet my mind after spending my entire life believing that all my random thoughts, bumping into each other in my mind, were important revelations that I had to listen to.

We meditated that day for eleven minutes—the longest eleven minutes of my life. But I didn't care. I was on a mission and I was convinced this strange new friend was my guide.

"Put your hands over your eyes. Open your eyes into the darkness of your hands. Stare at your palms as you slowly pull them away."

He looked at me, his face expressionless. He smiled from his eyes, a soothing smile, like Vera's voice so many years ago. "You are home, Jason."

He spoke again. "You have spent your life willing great things to happen. You have accomplished so much in the physical plane. You have learned the art of manifestation, through sheer will. Your mother's death freed you. Now we will teach you how to invest in trust. To be, not do. To surrender to that knowing inside you. That requires your being in NOW. That is what we will learn together."

He stood up and walked to the door. Then he paused, turned back and said, "You know what I am talking about, don't you?"

I did.

I had experienced this sort of familiarity with a new situation at various other times of my life, walking into a new place or meeting someone and knowing I was supposed to be there. Like the way Spanish had come so easily to me. The new words and meanings populating my mind like the ants in the ant farm from my kindergarten class. Or when I met Julio César Chávez and his brother. And, more recently, when I walked the concourse of the Universal Amphitheater with Michael. In all of those situations I had known I belonged. That's how I felt now.

So I did what I had done so many times before. I dove in, immersing myself in the learning.

I no longer saw Guru Singh as a robed wizard in a turban. Now he wasn't Merlin, but more like David Carradine's wise Chinese teacher in the TV series *Kung Fu*. Remember the teacher and lessons he would flash back to on his long walking journey?

After that first meeting, twice a week, every week, I sat cross-legged in front of Guru Singh and soaked it all in just like the little boy in *Kung Fu*. Listening, learning, asking questions, and then experiencing NOW through meditation.

I also meditated daily at home on my own. I converted a portion of my closet into a meditation area. On a small shelf I placed a candle, a small statue of Jesus that had been given to me as a child at my first communion, a picture of my mom and children, along with a quote by the Buddha that said, "Do not dwell in the past, do not dream of the future, concentrate the mind on the present moment."

Every morning and afternoon I went into the closet and smiled at the picture of my mom, realizing the irony of the courage it took for her to come out of the closet a decade before and tell me she was in love with Kim. I sat on an orange cushion purchased at Pier 1 Imports. I'd turn on some relaxing music and meditate for eleven minutes as Guru Singh had taught me.

In the beginning I fell into the trap most of us do. I did meditation—sitting there very sternly and seriously. I closed my eyes hard and actively pushed all the thoughts out of my mind, which of course in the process generates new thoughts even more annoying than the original ones. Thoughts like "SHHHHHHH Jason," "No, go away, I'm not thinking right now, I'm meditating," and "I wonder if my hands are positioned correctly?" Added to the pain in my back and the cramp in my legs was the strange phenomenon that every time I sat down to meditate I suddenly had to pee!

Around this time I listened to an audio book by the Trappist monk and contemplative Father Thomas Keating. In it he described contemplation as "we do not deny or repress what is in our conscious thinking process. We simply accept the fact of whatever is there and go beyond it, not by effort, but by letting go of whatever is there." He goes on to explain that sometimes in meditation we may get only a glimpse of that letting go, only a tiny slice of beautiful surrender. In those moments we experience God. Maybe just for a few seconds and maybe more. Whatever duration is just fine, Father Keating says, because those few seconds are worth more than a full day of normal thinking.

To help myself I developed an image with which I would start my meditation. I would close my eyes, envisioning a wise-looking Chinese man, like Confucius, sitting on the bank in between a fork in the river, with the river running on either side of him.

Instead of water, the river was made up of thoughts. My thoughts. This wise Chinese man (my mind) simply looked at each thought as it floated by and said gently "hmm." A thought floating by ... "hmm" ... another ... "hmm." Never engaging or resisting. Calmly observing the presence and letting it pass by with a simple "hmm."

As silly as it sounds this imagery worked for me. It was a visual representation of the concept of non-attachment and surrender I could clearly understand. After a few moments of doing this I would settle into a peaceful state and enjoy a magnificent meditation. Over time those moments went from seconds to a minute and, with more practice, to more and more minutes.

When I asked Guru Singh how to deal with a thought I didn't like, he would say: "What do you do when you see a billboard you don't like? Do you take a picture and carry it around with you? No. You see it and then you drive on by."

* * *

At one of my afternoon classes he asked me if I did yoga. "No," I said as images of people contorting their bodies while walking on their hands played in my head.

"Well, let's have you start with two poses, downward dog and paint-the-aura." He stood to demonstrate. Downward dog—a bit like a bear crawl without the crawling; and paint-the-aura—oddly similar to the dance moves in Willow Smith's "Whip My Hair" video. If you haven't seen it, Google it now so you can appreciate my clever wit.

When I returned later that week for my next session, Guru Singh asked me if I had done the postures. "No," I replied, feeling like high-school Jason sitting in Mr. Allen's class being called out for not doing the homework.

"Why not?" he asked. There was no judgment in his voice, only an innocent curiosity and intrigue.

The truth was I hadn't tried the postures because I thought they looked stupid. I hadn't done a bear crawl since high school football, and flopping my body up and down like Will Smith's daughter just wasn't what I was down for. It felt lame.

Not wanting to offend him, I gave an inoffensive answer: Okay, okay, I thought, then said, "I guess I was just a little lazy."

He closed his eyes and seemed to drift away, far away. I sat there wondering what was going on. I would later learn that Guru Singh closed his eyes like this from time to time to listen to the moment, to clear out any judgment or bias, and to understand what the moment is saying in order to convey it.

He opened his eyes. "No," he said, "everything I have learned about you is that you are NOT lazy. Lazy men don't make it here. They don't accomplish what you have." He paused. "Perhaps it was Guru Singh who was lazy. I didn't properly explain to you what the yoga postures are for. Men like you don't do things they don't find value in. So let me explain it now."

I don't know why this surprised me. Not only had the teacher taken responsibility for the student not doing his homework, but he also put into words what I was too afraid to say or didn't realize myself. He was right. I hadn't done the yoga not because I was lazy or because it looked lame. I didn't do it because I didn't see the value. It appeared to be a waste of time and so I skipped it like all the other waste-of-time things people had tried to make me do in my life.

"Yoga," he began, "is one methodology allowing you to stretch into your body, your body glove. It's like a glove or a pair of shoes: if it doesn't fit, it doesn't serve and if it doesn't serve, nothing works well. I asked you to do downward dog because it's the same exercise almost every animal does. Dogs do it after getting up from every nap. Stretching into the body glove enables the occupant of the body to fully utilize the body.

"Yoga has been developed over thousands of years to help you get in touch with those places in your physical form that generate emotional sensations, which in turn produce thought. It is getting to those places that allows us to ultimately have not only a body that fits, but a life that fits. When the body and the life fit, neither one of them disrupts your ability to have a clear sensation of God at all times. So in the midst of yoga we get into postures, we have movements and, equally important, we breathe consciously."

All of a sudden the lame yoga postures didn't seem so lame. In fact, yoga sounded like a really smart thing to do. I listened as the guru continued.

"I asked you to do downward dog because there's a relationship between the glands and organs of the abdomen and this relationship is effective when there is room for the glands and organs to relate. Inverting the body in downward dog releases the compression that takes place throughout our lives by sitting and standing. This increased space allows everything to move and function effectively.

"Also, I asked you to paint the aura. Kirlian photographs of the bodies of living creatures show there is an electromagnetic field that surrounds every one of us. This is what is known as the aura. When you do the exercise to paint the aura, you are actually spreading your intention into this electromagnetic field through the nerve endings in your hands. Each of our hands has 72,000 nerve endings, the same number in each of our feet. Reflexology is a therapy that utilizes this fact. It knows that these nerve endings connect to all of the glands and organs throughout our body and that we can affect those glands and organs by massaging the nerve endings. By the same fact, in reverse, we can affect the space around us by allowing the energy coming from our glands and organs through those nerve endings to be painted into the surrounding space. This may sound like woo-woo, but it is as real as a surgeon's scalpel.

"When I first met you, you told me you wanted to know God. If there is ever anything in life that you want to know, you have to go to a place where what you want to know has a relationship. When a bloodhound is being trained to find someone, they will take a piece of clothing the person has worn for the bloodhound to get the scent. The point of reference to discover God is the self within the self. Not the stories that the self has generated; not the beliefs that someone has propagated; but the unaltered self that sits at the core of each one of us. That's the trailhead on the path to knowing God. One methodology, amongst many methodologies, for discovering that trailhead to the self within the self is Kundalini yoga. Two of the postures in Kundalini yoga that I strongly recommend for this beginning stage are downward dog and painting the aura."

Now properly schooled in the science of yoga and understanding its value on my path, I decided to learn. In addition to my twice-weekly private classes, I would attend Guru Singh's weekly yoga class at Yoga West in Los Angeles.

There each week, Guru Singh would stand in front of one hundred or so students and talk about what he called Humanology. Our history. The reason we are here. That we are teaching masters. That we have a mission. That we are all one.

Then he would teach yoga. Not *do* yoga, but teach it. Posture by posture, explaining the reasons behind each one—what was being stretched, what took place in our bodies as a result, and how that would positively impact our lives. Through his stories, wit, and passion, yoga became a part of my life. Not just an activity, but a trusted friend with whom I began my day.

My favorite part of these public classes was the grand finale. Yes, the yoga class had a grand finale! Not an ending or a goodbye but a full-on spiritual climax.

Guru Singh would take his guitar, and a motley crew of musicians wearing yoga gear would join him on the small stage in the front of the class. Then they would jam, like those old videos of '60s' rock stars jamming with each other. They played the way rockers used to jam when musicians still had fun. Instead of long hair and songs of sex, drugs, and rock and roll, this yoga jam session featured white robes, ancient yogic chants, and messages of love and oneness … oh, and one hell of a front man, Guru Singh, strumming his guitar while his sterling silver bracelets created their own rhythm section and his turban bounced around like a dancing Sesame Street Elmo.

Many of these classes became family affairs—my wife, kids, nephews, everyone—positioned in the back corner of the class while Guru Singh taught and winked at us to let us know he was watching. It was one of my life's true treasures to learn and share this experience with my family. Not waiting to pass it on, but sharing real time, in the moment, creating our story together.

Putting what we learned in class into practice, we began a daily 6:30 a.m. yoga time in our home. Instead of starting the day with email or TV or arguments, we committed as a family to stretch into the day … literally. Seven or eight simple postures the whole family could do and enjoy, followed by a meditation.

As a family we were unwinding our physical bodies, connecting to a place of peace and well-being inside ourselves and creating a new family story. In health we are often taught that you are what you eat. I have found the same is true for other areas of our life—you are what you do and your daily practice sets the tone for your day.

* * *

Vera had taught me to understand how I formed. Why I thought the things I thought. Why my life had played out as it had. She clarified the physical and mental me, and helped me quiet my mind for this next stage of life.

With my mind quiet for the first time, Guru Singh was teaching me to widen my perspective and stretch into the window of my soul—the true me, beyond my primary scenario, beyond the paint can, and beyond the myth I had told of Jason.

Each meditation, each stretch of my body, each second of peace brought with it a glimpse of a true me I had never experienced. My two questions—Who am I? and Who is God?—were on a collision course. They had started as independent ideas, two logical trains of thought that were now merging into one.

I didn't know the answer yet, but I could now see the path. For the first time I was beginning to understand what my life would look like if the paint can of my brain was filled with white. In meditation, I was experiencing a glimpse of that peaceful, clear world, a world untainted by the programming of my youth.

And I wanted more.

·19·

SHAOLIN TEMPLE WITH THE DRAGON

I LOOKED UP IN FRONT OF ME. THROUGH THE MIST TOWERED A GIANT statue. A metallic monk peered out above the treetops, his hands pressed together, blessing the passage of all those lucky enough to make this journey.

I stopped and turned to the group of people who made this trip with me. There was something I needed to say. Not so much to them, maybe I was talking to myself. I spoke nonetheless.

"Whatever each of us has done," I said, not sure where these words were coming from. "Whatever has happened in our lives, however it is that we've each arrived here, it's all perfect. It's all okay. We're here … ."

With a tear of great joy in my eye, I entered the grounds of the Shaolin Temple in the foothills of the Songshan mountain range of China.

Two months prior, at the recommendation of David Wolfe, I had gone to see Ron Teeguarden, the master herbalist, who had asked me to meet him at his Beverly Hills store.

I arrived and walked through the door, the small Chinese bells on the door gently announcing my arrival. The store was filled with tinctures and plastic bottles of herbs, like an herbal pharmacy. Bottles with weird names I didn't yet know, but soon would.

I introduced myself and asked the man behind the register where I could find Ron. I followed him through the store, around the corner. We entered the tonic bar decorated with Chinese antiques, TV sets showing videos of Ron on expeditions searching for herbs, and large canisters filled with giant roots suspended in liquid, like herbal lava lamps. The bar looked like a Chinese version of the many hip Hollywood bars in the area. There were no daytime drunks, however, no pick-up lines, and no expensive bottles of champagne. Instead of coming to drink away your blues, this is where people came to tonify their lives. I'll explain that soon.

We continued past the bar into what looked like the herbal workshop of a mad scientist. It was. Glass canisters lined the shelves around the room, filled with roots, leaves, stems, berries, and other treasures I couldn't yet identify.

"Hi," Ron said. He was a tall man, really tall. I'm 6'3" and he was taller. His white hair sprouted up in patches around his head and face, making him look a bit like a bearded dragon.

He smiled a crooked smile as if sensing the amazement I was feeling in this herbal wonderland. I looked closely at him. It was like that moment in *Back to the Future*, when Marty meets Christopher Lloyd's character, Dr. Brown, for the first time. As Ron began to share his herbal philosophy with me, I was only half listening. My brain was busy deciding what to make of this fascinating man, wondering if he was some crazy doctor hawking snake oil or my new guide.

"Have a seat," Ron said interrupting my ponderings. "Ya... so welcome. It's nice to meet you."

There was an awkward feeling that's hard to explain. It wasn't as though I wasn't supposed to be there, but more like we had a purpose, a history together, and the awkwardness came from having to get all the usual small talk out of the way so we could get down to business; or better stated, down to life.

"Thank you for seeing me," I started off. "David spoke so highly of you. In fact, what he said was, 'you have to consume Chinese herbs, and to do that right you have to see Ron Teeguarden.'"

Ron smiled his crooked smile. His eyes shifted nervously as if he wasn't entirely comfortable with the compliment. There was something endearing about this man, like a long lost uncle who had traveled the world and had come home to share his adventures.

I told him my story just as I had told Michael and Vera and David and Guru Singh before him. The whole story from the beginning to the present. Then I said, "I'm here because I want to learn. David told me there is an intelligence to the herbs, a special quality you can feel in your body. I want to experience that feeling. "Will you teach me?"

This is where my herbal education began.

"Chinese herbs," Ron said, "will become your new best friend. They saved my life. They will change yours."

He looked at me as if he wanted to say something else, but wasn't sure he should. Then he spoke:

"I want you to know that what you're feeling is temporary. The exhaustion. That is your Jing, your life force; it's been depleted, spent throughout the life you have described. It's why you are here." He paused, looked at me, and then he continued: "There is something special in you. You are going to do something special with all of this you are learning. I will help you restore your Jing. When that is done there will be no stopping you."

I sat there amazed, the hair on my arms standing up.

He told me his story. How as a college student he had a viral infection that doctors couldn't diagnose or cure. He was wiped out, aching and depressed. He lost 50 pounds. Hopeless, he contemplated ending it all until a friend, returning from Canada, brought him some bottles of a Chinese supplement containing an herb called He Shou Wu. Ron was in such bad shape that he didn't read the dosage instructions properly, and instead of taking a tablespoon three times per day, he drank it by the bottle. He got better. His energy returned almost immediately. In a short time he was back to normal. It was a miracle ... a miracle in that it motivated this man to begin a journey of discovery, learning, and teaching that would bring Chinese herbs to the West.

In the late 1970s Ron met his mentor and great Taoist Master, Sung

Jin Park.

Ron would spend the next several years learning at the feet of his great teacher and friend. Just as I had learned Spanish translating Mexican pop songs, Ron would learn the art of herbalism by translating Master Park's teachings.

Now, 35 years later, I was sitting with a great teacher, just as he had so many years before. Only Ron the student was now the teacher, sharing his experience with a new student: me.

We talked for hours. I was fascinated by this man and intrigued by his knowledge and description of the herbs. They weren't things to him. They were like fairies with which he played and through which he created magical potions.

He explained the ancient Chinese philosophy of the three treasures—Jing (life force), Qi (vitality) and Shen (spirit), and the balancing characteristics of Yin (conservation) and Yang (fire)—and how they all interact in the body, each like a player on a basketball team. He told me that a good herbal formula can keep you balanced just like a good tune-up keeps your car running well.

The most important lesson that day and what had the greatest impact on me was Ron's explanation of health, what he called Radiant Health and described as "health beyond danger." He explained we can nourish our bodies and souls to the point that we are no longer in danger from the risks of our daily life. Instead of obsessing about how to eliminate all the toxins, chemicals, and pollution from our world (a truly impossible task), we tonify our bodies; we strengthen them through diet, exercise, meditation, and herbs until we reach the point of Radiant Health—health beyond danger.

Then he answered the question: "Yes, I will teach you."

Ron pointed to a canister with large burnt-red, glossy mushrooms in it. "Those are Reishi mushrooms," he said. "There are many great herbs, but none greater than Reishi. Reishi is a powerful immune builder that also opens your spirit to the heavens. In Chinese temples there are giant murals depicting heaven. At the top, there is always a Reishi mushroom. Someday you will go to China with me and we will find one. When you do you will know you have found your way."

This is how I ended up in China, at the Shaolin Temple, as part of my education with my new teacher, Ron Teeguarden.

I had been consuming Chinese herbs for about two months when we arrived at the Shaolin Temple. I say consuming, not taking, because they are plants. When we say taking, it conjures up thoughts of a pharmaceutical medicine to treat something. The tonic herbs, herbs that promote the Radiant Health Ron taught me about, are plants. Wild, intelligent, special plants that promote health and well-being. Maybe the best way to explain it is to say we consume the herbs so we don't have to TAKE medicine. Yeah, I like that.

Sixty days after adding these special plants to my diet, I joined Ron and a small group of his friends on the trip to China. The Shaolin Temple is an extraordinary place. It's the Chinese birthplace of three modalities—Zen Buddhism, Kung fu, and Herbal Medicine. These are the three divisions of the temple, the three arts practiced daily by the monks who live there.

Imagining a Shaolin monk is almost impossible until you meet one. They are the most humble, sincere, sweetest beings I have ever met. Yet with a deep breath and a lightning-quick strike they are also the fiercest of warriors. This is the unique mix of the Shaolin training, a mastery of the body and mind through Buddhist teachings and meditation combined with kung fu and tai chi.

For me, the temple combined two parts of my life I thought were incompatible—the scrappy fighter who clawed his way up the ladder and the calm, loving, spiritual being I was uncovering through my new diet, yoga, and meditation. At Shaolin I saw them combined, two parts of the whole.

I spent the week learning tai chi, meditating, and studying with the senior monks of the temple.

The monks' discipline is impressive. Beginning with an early morning wake up, their day is spent disciplining the mind and body through physical and mental workout and service toward others.

I don't know why I didn't sleep much at the temple. I was calm. It wasn't that I was excited like a kid at Disneyland. I just didn't feel the need to sleep much. I got up each morning, did yoga and meditated, and then walked the grounds barefoot, soaking in the sacred energy of the temple's earth.

It was such a special experience to watch the monks chanting and meditating and to see the young children practicing kung fu. I felt like I had a backstage pass to a secret world that no one back home knew existed. And I was always looking for the Reishi mushrooms Ron told me about.

In my morning meditations I found myself crying. Not a sad cry. No, there was no sadness at all. More, it was a cry of awe, of the sheer wonder of life. I had a question … a thought … stuck in my head. "How did I get here?"

I had spent my entire life climbing, with each step leading logically to the next. Even if my life didn't make sense to others, to me it did. I'd been poor, so I sold gum to buy lunch. I liked selling things so I got a job at the flea market. There I learned to sell more things to more people. Many of the people spoke Spanish, which was a barrier for me. I learned Spanish by translating music. Having learned to sell, to speak Spanish, and to appreciate the music, I became a Spanish-language concert promoter. Realizing that market was a niche, I expanded into English music. Then I rode the wave as high as I could.

See what I mean? Totally logical.

Now here I was, meditating under a tree, on the grounds of a sacred Buddhist temple, on the very site where Zen Buddhism began in China.

The very earth where many of the herbs I consumed grew.

How in the fuck did I get here?

And so I cried. A cry of desperation, tears of wonderment spilling from my heart. Why am I here?

The trip was magical. We were guided around the temple and grounds by a monk named Li Bo. Li Bo was a tiny man with a kind, gentle demeanor—like the monks in the movie *Crouching Tiger, Hidden Dragon*. He spoke broken English, but it was good enough for us to bond. He was a basketball fan. I had season tickets and kept him entertained with stories of Kobe Bryant, Laker games, and watching the team win the NBA Championship. In exchange he taught me about Shaolin. Together we searched for Reishi mushrooms.

One day, Li Bo told us we would be going to Bodhidharma's cave. Bodhidharma was the founder of the Shaolin tradition. He was an Indian Buddhist monk who traveled to China and arrived at the Shaolin monastery. When they refused him entry he retreated to this cave high in the mountains where, legend says, he meditated for nine long years. He stayed there so long that birds nested on his head and his aura was burned into the side of the wall. After nine years he came down from the cave to deliver the Shaolin Buddhist and kung fu teachings, which are still taught today.

Where is the cave? To answer that question, Li Bo pointed up (I mean way up) to the highest point on the mountain and said, "A little past there."

I'm not a dramatic guy. I don't like hyperbole. So take it at face value when I tell you that where he pointed, that far away mountaintop was … well … really really far away. I spoke for the group when I said, "We're going to walk there?"

"Yes," Li Bo said. "Or run if you want."

Turns out that the monks run this route every day, sometimes twice, once in the morning and once in the afternoon. I say run, but they don't really run, they float. "Come on, Jason," you're probably thinking. If you doubt me, Google it and you'll see what I mean. Touching only their toes for brief seconds, they seem to float as they run along from step to step. If they feel they need a little more challenge that day, they bear crawl down—all the monks, young and old, every day.

"How long is it going to take?" someone asked.

"Maybe two hours," Li Bo said, "for you guys. When I run I can get there in 12 minutes."

!!@#&!*

We set out to the cave in the sky. We held a steady pace trying to keep up with Li Bo. Soon the group had splintered as everyone found their own pace. Li Bo, Ron's son Lucky, Reverend Michael Beckwith (a longtime client and friend of Ron's), and I were the first to arrive at the final leg of the journey: a multi-leveled series of 1,000 hand-formed stone stairs that led straight up to the cave.

"Do you want to run?" Li Bo asked innocently.

What could we say? "Yes, let's do it," I said for the group.

So there we were, like a corny joke told at a banquet—a monk, a concert promoter, a reverend, and a kid named Lucky—running up the stairs to Bodhidharma's cave. Let me clarify this. As I already said, Li Bo floated to the top. Lucky, Michael, and I tried our best to run, navigating the tiny stone steps with uneven rises in the scorching Chinese sun.

As we were reaching the top we looked down to admire the journey that got us here. Far in the distance below us, below the blue sky and clouds, beyond the endless mountains and trees, sat the Shaolin Temple where we had begun the day. Now we were a couple of steps from the cave. It was beautiful ... a perfect analogy for my life. I closed my eyes and, as Guru Singh had taught me, listened to the moment.

Then we heard a voice, "Hey guys." Coming up the final flight of stairs behind us was Olivia, a young client of Ron's. She'd recently had a portion of her leg removed after a tumor was discovered in it. This trip was her inspiration to make it through that ordeal, to recover, to make it here. We stood off to the side and the girl with one good leg led the way.

When we arrived at the cave, we noticed an inscription in a stone arch above the entrance.

"Place of silent mystery," Li Bo said, sensing our question.

We entered, held hands, and Reverend Beckwith led us in prayer.

Li Bo took us up one more flight of stairs to an observation point above the cave. There, sitting on the ground as if waiting for me to arrive, was a small Chinese man selling Reishi mushrooms. It was surreal. I'd been waiting to find Reishi, just as Ron had described on that first day when he told me about this trip. I'd looked everywhere and now here, in the most unlikely of locations, I found them. I bought one for each member of our group and gave them out as each arrived at the top.

When Ron arrived, I handed him the most perfect Reishi I had found. I felt tears well up in my eyes. I looked at him and said, "I've spent the whole trip wondering why I'm here. And just like the painting of heaven we found Reishi way up here, in our heaven."

Then Ron repeated the words that Vera had uttered in our first meeting, the words Guru Singh's eyes had silently conveyed to me: "You are home, Jason."

I breathed, sat down, looked out from my own little slice of heaven, and we meditated. One by one the group arrived and joined me, each of us with our own story of how we came to this place, united by the Reishi mushrooms we held in our hands and the piece of Shaolin embedded in our hearts.

A few weeks after we returned from the temple I went to see Ron. I had saved a couple extra Reishi mushrooms and Ron had promised we would make a special tea with them. He got out a large pot. Together we broke the Reishi into pieces and placed them in the pot. Each piece carried with it a memory of our magical journey to the top of the mountain. Then Ron pointed to canisters and jars. Taking handfuls, he told me a story about each herb and then added it to the pot. "Gynostemma is the supreme longevity herb," he said. "Drink it every day." Into the pot. "Ginseng root is very special, Jason. After 15 years of life a ginseng root has a gene that activates and the root won't die. Ginseng lives on and on. This one is 25 years old. It found me. Now that intelligence will go into our tea." Into the pot. "Licorice root is the great harmonizer. It facilitates the combining of the essence and flavor of the herbs." Into the pot.

This was how Ron taught me, on that day and on many, many others—in impromptu classes disguised as chance meetings, consultations, and tea making.

Once we had assembled the perfect combination of herbs, Ron told me he would brew it all night and that I should come back tomorrow. The next day was my daughter's birthday and we would share the tea with her.

The next day I returned, eager to drink our special tea made from the Reishi mushroom from the Shaolin Temple. The mushroom that found me and helped me to find myself.

We arrived to see Ron standing proudly over a teapot. He was waiting for us. He had invited our friend, Wang Bo, another Shaolin monk, to join us. I sensed he was feeling the same anticipation I was.

Then something amazing happened, as if that Reishi mushroom wanted to make a point and give a demonstration of the awesome intelligence of the herbs. The door to the herb shop swung open and in walked Reverend Michael Beckwith. He had no idea we were there, or what we were doing. He had come to buy his monthly supply of herbs and walked in on our gathering.

So there we were, all together. We sang "Happy Birthday" to Nataly. Michael said a prayer. Then we drank our magical tea with the mushroom that had called us to China to find it and then brought us all back to LA to find each other. A lesson taught by a sacred herb to her lucky students.

·20·

JENNI RIVERA, A DRIVE-BY, AND A WHITE ROSE

WE HAD A LOT IN COMMON. WE HAD BOTH BEEN SINGLE PARENTS. She had begun her career selling music at a flea market in Los Angeles, just as I had begun at the flea market in San Jose. We were two scrappers who made it in the music business against all odds. It was fun to compare stories and talk about how blessed we were.

After leaving Live Nation, I vowed to take a break, to clear my head and not jump back in, which is what I did.

That is, until Jenni Rivera called. She had recently parted ways with her concert booking manager and was looking for some advice from a friend who knew a thing or two about the music business. She asked me to be an advisor.

For those of you who don't know who Jenni Rivera was, or only know her because you saw her memorial on TV, she was a huge star. A once-in-a-lifetime combination of talent rolled into one feisty, in-your-face, sass machine. She could kick your ass in one moment and melt your heart in the next. She was the Spanish-language equivalent of Janis Joplin's voice and the Kardashians real-life drama combined with Gene Simmons' business savvy and Sandra Bullock's lovability.

Trying to manage her, any part of her, was, well, impossible. In truth I was one of her many friends, on a long list of people who loved her. She called me her booking manager, but I was just a guy she called for advice now and then when she wanted to tour the United States or get another perspective on an issue.

On Thursday, December 6, 2012, I went to meet with Jenni at a small Mexican restaurant in Encino, California. When I arrived the manager showed me to a booth where Jenni sat in a velour sweatsuit and a rhinestone-embroidered baseball cap. She was leaving for Mexico the next day and had asked to meet to catch up on business, but more importantly it seemed, to talk about life.

The prior September we'd had a big success together, selling out two nights at the Universal Amphitheater in Hollywood and grossing over $1 million, a record for her in the U.S. We parlayed that into a four-concert deal for 2013. Had those shows played out it would have put her in elite status in the concert business.

But Jenni already lived amongst the elite. She was a superstar with down-home likeability. She presided over her two million-plus Twitter followers with her unique humor, in-your-face style, and humility. Through her many reality TV shows the public lived with Jenni and she was part of their family. Like your crazy aunt, you never knew what she would do next.

So that day I showed up, as with most meetings with Jenni, not knowing what to expect. She was excited. ABC had decided to move forward with an English-language TV show she and her longtime business partner, Pete, were developing. "I'm blowing up, J," she said with a sassy smile. "Soon you won't be able to get hold of me."

Still, she was sad. Her marriage had recently failed and she was, like all of us, dealing with family issues. She, like I had, found herself once again a single parent and was trying to sort through life and love on her own.

We shared all our stories that day. It was an odd feeling I couldn't put words to, as though we just had to say everything. We sat and talked and talked. At one point after I gave her some advice she deemed a little too woo-woo, she smiled and said, "Can't a diva and her white boy just go on a drive-by and solve it the old fashioned way?!" It was her way of breaking the tension, saying we were friends and expressing exasperation with another divorce. After lunch, as we pulled up to her house, I gave her a hug and she looked at me.

"You know, J, sometimes things get really tough and I think maybe I should just quit. Then I hug my kids, talk to a friend, or tweet with my fans, and I can't believe how much they love me. It's like no matter how crazy my life gets they love me more. It almost scares me. Like, what's gonna happen to me next ...."

That was the last time I saw my friend alive. A few days later, leaving Monterrey, Mexico after a concert, her plane went down. With it went all the dreams and hopes of a superstar.

Her family, Pete, and I produced a memorial for her fans on December 19 at the Universal Amphitheater, the venue she had sold out a few months before. It was one of those events for which words can't do justice. The venue was packed, standing room only, as her fans came to say goodbye. On the stage sat her mom and dad, her brothers and sisters, nieces and nephews, her five children, and her baby granddaughter.

One by one her family and friends told stories of her youth, of her generosity, and of her love. Her 11-year-old son summed it up best. Standing on stage, tears in his eyes, he said simply, "It's a real honor to say that Jenni Rivera, the person everyone is talking about, is my mom … and she still lives in me."

At the end of the memorial I stood at the rear of the stage, watching Jenni's family, friends, and fans place single white roses on her red casket. I took a deep breath and I cried, truly cried for the first time that day. I missed my friend. I felt for her family. I agonized for her children.

I wondered how this could all be possible. I questioned my own life. The work with Vera and Guru Singh, meditation, yoga, all of it. What did it all mean if life could end in an instant?

As tears streamed harder and harder down my face, I found the answer. Jenni's gift that day, to us all, was a reminder to live every moment, not like it's our last—no, that's not how Jenni lived. Her message was to live each moment like it's our first.

So I left to do just that.

·21·

MINT CHOCOLATE CHIP, MARRIAGE, AND A MIRACLE

WHEN I MET CHRISTY THE FIRST TIME IT WAS INNOCENT. A MUTUAL friend said with a slip of the tongue, or a psychic insight, "You need to be with him," and grabbed Christy's hand to introduce us.

Our eyes met. A spark. A big spark. Then we started talking. Not, "Hi, what's your name?" No, we skipped right to the good stuff—life story, dreams, the kind of juicy details you usually save for dessert.

I will be totally honest. I had never met a woman like this. We were both in relationships so it wasn't sexual. Okay, let me clarify that. She was sexy, deeply sexy—tall, slender, brown hair, and gorgeous blue eyes. But there was more, something different. She had depth, intelligence, super femininity, but with a strength and passion, like dark chocolate in real mint ice cream. Not the kind you buy at the supermarket freezer, but like homemade ice cream, rich and creamy, deep and complex, mixed with the zing and POW to your taste buds of real mint. You know what I mean? Can you taste it?

I could. But like I said, we were in relationships so that was that, right? Apparently the universe, and my daughter, had other things in mind.

A few months later I was single. One day talking with Nataly she asked me, "Dad, do you remember that lady we met at the health conference?"

"Dr. Christy?" I said.

"Yeah," she replied. "What did you think of her?"

Nataly had been there in that ice cream moment; she'd seen the spark.

"She's amazing," I said. "That's the kind of woman I want to meet."

Nataly giggled. "Dad," she said with the innocence of a small child about to tell their Daddy a really big secret.

"Yes, Nataly."

"When you met her, Dr. Christy, I knew something. I felt something, like a vision, except I didn't see it. I just knew it."

"What?" I asked her. "What did you know?"

"When we came home I told Kevin that I had met Daddy's new wife."

Now to understand my reaction to this, let me tell you a story about my daughter Nataly. One time when she was five or six we were outside our house. She was riding her little tricycle, wearing her cute little pink glasses, riding up and down the street yelling, "Catch me Daddy ... catch me Daddy!"

All of a sudden out of the corner of my eye I saw a little boy standing in the middle of the street. I told Nataly to stay put and I rushed over to pick him up. I held the boy and walked to the sidewalk. His mother came running from a nearby house. He had wandered into the street. She thanked me profusely, the way one does in those types of situations.

"Perfect, now back to Nataly," I thought. Except Nataly was sitting there on the curb, her little glasses flooded with tears and a look of pure disgust on her face.

I went to give her a hug and she pushed me away.

"What's wrong?" I asked her.

"That little boy," she snarled. "He's not yours. I am."

My heart melted. I felt her jealousy, so I tried to be logical.

"Well, he was all alone in the middle of the street. Don't you think it was a good idea for Daddy to save him before he got hit by a car?"

"NO!" Nataly said. "I hate him!"

That's a story Nataly and I have laughed about many times over the years. But the truth has always remained that Nataly never really approved of anyone I dated. They just weren't good enough for her Daddy.

So for Nataly to have met a woman, had a feeling she was my wife, AND proclaim this to her brother was an almost impossible story for me to believe.

I yelled for Kevin to come up.

"Ya." He was fourteen and "ya" was one of the few words he spoke at the time.

"What did Nataly tell you about a woman named Dr. Christy we met at the health conference?" I asked him.

"I dunno," he said.

"Think about it."

"Oh … ya … she said she met your wife or something like that. Said she was an amazing lady and we should do a set-up like in that stupid *Parent Trap* movie … can I go now?" he spit this out in one monotone sentence.

I looked at Nataly, squinting my eyes as if trying to see a different angle of what was going on.

"Call her, Dad. I think she likes you."

I tracked down a mutual friend who had her number and sent her a text. You know the kind. "Hey, we met, hope you remember me, how are you, blah blah blah." A day went by and no answer. I sent another one and another day and no answer.

My male ego kicked in. All I wanted was a response. Good, bad, whatever. Then I stopped myself; maybe I have the wrong number. I reached out to my friend again and asked her to contact Christy and see what was up.

Soon a text from Christy came. We set up a call. Then a date. And well, the rest is history.

But I'll tell you the story anyway.

Christy was living in San Diego at the time with her daughter Jadyn. I'd been taking flying lessons and asked her to pick me up at a small airport near her home. I got my instructor and a small plane and off I went to my first date with the mint-chocolate-chippy woman named Dr. Christy.

That first date was simple and beautiful, just like every other moment of our relationship from that point forward. We walked on the beach for hours. Drinking green juices and catching up. I say catching up because the sensation was we had known each other forever. We were like two people who played together as kids and had now reunited. We just had a little catching up to do.

The entire day can be summarized by the beautiful words Christy said. Walking hand-in-hand, barefoot down the beach, she looked into my eyes and said, "I knew the moment I saw you that I was made to love you. I didn't understand why we were both in relationships. That's why I didn't answer your first text. I couldn't stand the thought of not being with you. I have always loved you, Jason."

I know you may read that and think it's too forward or maybe even crazy. But it made perfect sense to me. There was a deep knowing inside, like all those other times in my life.

I was home.

Not long after I went to see Guru Singh. I told him about Christy, about Nataly's vision, and about the date.

He closed his eyes, like I told you he sometimes does. His eyes were closed longer than usual, almost as if he was savoring the moment.

When he opened his eyes he pointed to a framed newsprint picture. It was of a woman, sitting in a field. An angelic woman in white in a field of green.

"Do you see that picture?" he asked me.

I nodded and he continued.

"I was flying home from India one day and I found that picture in a magazine. It caught my eye. No, it spoke to me. 'This is your wife.' I heard the voice just like I hear you today. This made no sense to me in the moment, but even then, so many years ago, I had learned to trust. I ripped out the picture and took it with me.

"I did some research and that picture is actually a painting. At the time the painting was one hundred years old. The woman had lived another hundred years before that. Now none of it made any sense at all. But still the picture spoke to me. 'This is your wife.'

"A few weeks later I was at a yoga festival. I was walking through the crowd and caught a glimpse of a beautiful woman, dressed all in white, sitting in a grass field, a real-life mirror of the magazine picture I had been carrying in my pocket. I knew in that moment she was the one ... but I had a problem."

What a beautiful story, I thought. What could possibly be the problem?

He continued, "I am a yogi, not a player. I didn't know what to say to her. A while later my teacher, Yogi Bhajan, called for me. I went to see him and he asked, 'Guru Singh, have you met anyone new lately?'

"You see he knew my wife, Guruperkarma, before I did. He met her at a gathering in Canada. When he met her he knew she was to be my wife, he just didn't know how yet. That day he wasn't asking me if I had met ANYONE. His real question was had I met THE ONE. My wife.

"At that point, I hadn't met her. I had only seen her. Later that night

Yogi Bhajan made sure we were in the same place at the same time, and that the answer to his question would be 'Yes, I have met someone.'

"When we returned to Los Angeles from the conference, Yogi Bhajan said to me, 'Guru Singh, she is your wife. Call her and ask her to marry you.'

"So I did. And do you know what, Jason? She told me that when the phone rang she knew who it was and what I was calling for.

"Forty years later. Hmm. Well, we are one soul occupying two bodies. That is what is happening with you. Christy is your wife."

We ended the day with a big hug and three simple words from my Guru: "Bring her here."

A couple of weeks later, after a few more dates and getting to know Jadyn (who with the simplistic depth of a child told me, "Thank you for being my mommy's soul mate"), Christy and I arrived together at Guru Singh's house.

We all sat down. He smiled the smile of a father who knows his son has found the one.

We talked for a moment. Then Guru Singh said simply, "So when is it?"

"When is what?" I asked.

"When is the date that we will formalize that which already is?" he said in the odd phrasing of a guru.

And that was that.

A couple of months later we were married in a small ceremony in the meditation room of our home.

Guru Singh, Guruperkarma, Nataly, Kevin, and Jadyn were there, along with our friend, the Shaolin monk Wang Bo, who doubled as the photographer.

The wedding was simple yet elegant. Not elegant like fancy. No. In fact we did nothing to decorate or create any external pizzazz. It was a from-the-heart kind of elegance, a family formalizing a bond that had existed always.

In a touching moment we placed a Zen garden, a small box of sand, in the middle of the floor. We each placed something in the garden that represented who we were in the family. Kevin put in a turtle to represent his love of animals, his autonomy in caring for them, and the role of his family in supporting this love. Nataly placed a jade heart to represent love and understanding, Jadyn added a small statue of the Buddha sitting under the Bodhi tree as a symbol that all of our dreams can come true. Christy placed a green apple in the garden representing a healthy and vibrant family. I went last and put a small tattered statue of Winnie the Pooh. My grandma had given it to me years prior with a card. On the card there was a picture of Pooh and Piglet walking together. "Pooh," said Piglet. "Yes, Piglet," answered Pooh. "Nothing, I just wanted to be sure you were there."

I was no longer alone. I had found my playmate, the one I had been looking for since the days of sitting by myself in the corner at my mom's work. The one I had longed for as I charged up the hill of life trying so hard to succeed ... trying so hard to be loveable.

The irony of it all is that my partner turned out to be the person who said those beautiful words to me on the beach. "I was born to love you." No hard work, no compromise, no struggle, no prerequisites. A simple truth. "I was born to love you."

A few days after our wedding Wang Bo called me. He sounded excited. He needed to see me.

When he arrived he pulled out the photographs he had taken of our wedding. They were beautiful. Moments of love captured through the lens of a monk. Then he showed me the last photo, a picture of Christy and me kissing at the moment of I DO. Reflecting right through our faces, as if in divine form, was the statue of the Buddha that sat in our meditation room. There we were, Christy and I, expressing our love, and there was the Buddha shining through our kiss. I asked Wang Bo if he had done some kind of special effect to the picture. "No," he said. He was visibly shaken. "This is how it came out. All the pictures on either side were normal. But this one, at that very moment: it was special."

A week later he told me he had sent the picture to his teachers at the Shaolin Temple, the most senior monks. They studied the picture and reported back to him. They said that our love, Christy's and mine, was deep. That it went back seven lifetimes. We had been together many times before. This picture was an expression of that. A blessing.

I love this story. So tender, just like the heart of a monk. If you ask me what I believe, I'll tell you. I believe we all see what we are putting out. We see the world through the lens of our consciousness. That special photograph is the result of our collective perspectives, from the love of everyone who nurtured us on our path to find each other, from the expression of love of a small family that came together in a meditation room for a wedding, and from the love of everyone whose life will be touched by seeing this beautiful snapshot of time.

Our wedding was not just of two people, but of a community of consciousness ... a guru and his wife; three beautiful children; a woman so delicious I describe her as ice cream; me, a man who had released the scared little boy inside him and found true love; and all this captured by a Buddhist monk whose lens is so pure that when he snapped the moment, his greatest symbol of love, the Buddha, reflected back, as if silently conveying a message to us all ...

"Love will always find the way."

·22·

COKE VERSUS PEPSI

ONE DAY WHILE ON VACATION, I WAS LOOKING OUT AT THE OCEAN AND checked my iPhone. I was always a BlackBerry man, but after I left Live Nation my emails went from several hundred down to a dozen or so and I decided to join the cool crowd and get an iPhone. I checked my phone and I had an email from one of Kevin's middle school teachers.

The message went something like this:

"Dear Mr. Garner: My name is Mrs. So-and-So. I'm your son's technology teacher. I am writing to you because I understand you're on vacation and I wanted to make you aware of a very serious issue involving your son in my class. He wrote a very disrespectful essay and I have alerted the school counselor, who is as concerned as I am. Please contact me."

Hmm. I wonder what that's all about? An essay in technology class? Isn't technology class a fancy name for computer lab? I replied, thanking Mrs. So-and-So for her message and asking her to please forward me the essay so I could see it.

Kevin, like his father, had been a stellar student throughout grade school. Great grades and delightful citizenship marks. The kid all the teachers liked. When he got into middle school he began to stretch into himself, as I had so many years before. More and more he was finding outside sources of education and questioning the value of what he was learning in school.

He became fascinated by marine life and so he volunteered at the local aquarium as a student docent. He loved dogs and cats and helped out at the Lange Foundation. He wanted to scuba dive and spent his summers at scuba camp exploring the ocean. This was his hands-on education, and he was thriving.

A day after her initial email to me, the technology teacher forwarded me the essay. The first thing that caught my attention was the subject matter: "Do you prefer Coke or Pepsi?" Apparently Mrs. So-and-So had shown the *Coke versus Pepsi: The Cola Wars* documentary in class. It was a story of how Coke and Pepsi had been battling each other for the money and minds of America. Then she asked the kids to write an essay on which soda they preferred and why.

By now you have gotten to know me a bit, so I don't think it will come as any surprise that I found this assignment to be total ... well ... horseshit. My son, the vegetarian, living in a house where we loved our bodies and consumed foods that showed it, was asked to write about soda? To write an essay about something that study after study has shown to contribute to childhood obesity and hyperactivity in students? A product that many responsible schools were banning from classrooms because of the negative health and behavior effects it had on children?

In the email the teacher explained to me that the superintendent had mandated that staff teach across subjects. She had decided to teach writing using *The Cola Wars* as the prompt.

I couldn't wait to read my son's essay, which had caused such a stir with Mrs. So-and-So and the school counselor. Here it is:

Do You Prefer Coke or Pepsi?

I prefer Coca-Cola because in my homeland, people prefer Coke. My homeland, which is Mexico, makes their Coke with cane sugar so it tastes super fantastic. Coke is like the bee's knees, if you know what I mean. If you ask me Pepsi tastes like the fecal matter of a cow. In my homeland, people smash Pepsi bottles on the ground because it tastes so bad.

My mom used to live in my homeland before she crossed the border and she smuggled some Mexican Coke over for me. She's the boss of sauce if you know what I mean. If you ask me she is a Mexi-can and not a mexi-can't. My mom is now a U.S. citizen so she can't be deported anymore. She owns a restaurant that sells Mexican Coca-Cola. It's the bee's knees if you know what I mean.

Okay, so my son has a tinge of Garner smart-ass in him. But what did the teacher expect, a serious reply? Is that even possible? I like Coke better because … um … the can is red? Most disturbing to me was that in a class of 30 students Kevin was the only one with the wit and original thinking to avoid walking in the narrow-minded path this well-meaning but … uh, let's just leave it at well-meaning … teacher had laid out for the students.

Kevin wrote a satire, an essay that mocked its subject matter, mocked the failed U.S. immigration policy that had hurt his mom and so many; and he even found a funny way to say cow poop. But because it didn't fit the norm, his work was deemed "shocking" and "disturbing." Like the assignment itself, I found the school's response, to quote my son, to be like the fecal matter of a cow.

The stupidity of this assignment planted a seed in our heads, a seed that sprouted the idea of a different way of learning. One in which students are allowed to follow their own path, to explore their passions, and to learn skills that will enrich their lives far beyond an in-depth exploration of the war between Coke and Pepsi. The seed was planted and now we would see what grew from it.

In September of that same year, Kevin entered high school. Our area high school is one of the best in the state and I had high hopes that Kevin would find inspiration there. However, by the end of the first quarter signs of boredom were appearing. His homework was not getting done, he seemed distant and lost, and "I dunno" was the best response I could get from him when I picked him up and asked about his day. I know many of you are thinking, "That sounds like every teenager." You're right. That's exactly the problem.

Our children are being educated in a system that looks largely the same as it did at the time of the Second World War, a system that was designed to prepare young men and women for a factory job on the great assembly lines of America. Ever notice the similarities? Bells ringing to alert children and workers when to move, cafeterias for meals, standardized everything and no reward for thinking outside the box.

This system worked when it matched the world, but now the world has changed many times since then. While it's changing right before our eyes, we keep educating our kids, the future's adults, in the same way we always have. It's not working.

How do we know? Like we know everything else: from TV.

One of my favorite examples is a commercial that runs during nearly all of the major sporting events. The ad features former college athletes who now work for Enterprise Rent-A-Car. They talk proudly about the sport they used to play, the university they attended, and the job they now hold at Enterprise. Then we're informed that Enterprise hires more new college graduates than ANY OTHER COMPANY.

I have nothing against Enterprise, but if we estimate that the average student leaves college with a $60,000 debt and that the average car rental employee makes $30,000, you don't need to be a college graduate to see the problem.

So we decided to do something different. We started our own school for our son in our home. Sounds complicated but it's not. It's simple and it's legal and in some cases (not all, but definitely ours), it was the right and necessary thing to do.

My son went from being bored, uninspired, and debating the attributes of Coke and Pepsi to an education that he directs and that teaches him in a way that elicits the passion inside. He took the lead in building his educational plan and we supported him.

He works with animals at an animal conservatory caring for tigers, cougars, eagles, and zebras. He's learning to interact with these beautiful creatures: what they eat, how they behave, how to help them ... does this sound like many teenagers you know?

He studies three days a week with a Zen Buddhist monk from the Shaolin Temple. He's learning the virtues of compassion, quiet mind, and yes, kung fu. Aren't those things we want our young people to learn?

Kevin learns psychology from a licensed psychologist. They are approaching the inner-workings of his mind in a fun way that has him learning while he grows as a young man. It's a lot better than waiting until a mid-life crisis, no?

He studies humanology. Not world history from a war-by-war perspective, but a true history of who we are, how we got here, and what a human being is truly capable of creating and experiencing. This is combined with meditation and yoga as he learns to stretch his body and mind. He's getting life skills versus memorization to pass a test.

Yes, he still learns the basics, which takes about an hour a day and can be done in a fun and interesting way.

Despite all this the number one question I get asked is, "Aren't you worried about his social skills?" Hmm. Lets think about that one together. In order to do so, let's close our eyes and think back to high school and the social lessons we learned.

Snitches get stitches ...

Roll it, lick it and smoke it ...

Come on baby, you know I love you ...

Nerd, dweeb, geek, slut, pimple face ...

And now in today's world add armed guards protecting students from the other students who have been bullied to the breaking point.

I'm not saying that nothing good comes from high school. I'm not saying that sometimes kids don't teach each other good lessons. But many times, for so many kids, the downside of the educational system far outweighs the positive.

Peer pressure is not limited to students. How many of us as parents have given in to something because we want to be seen as good parents? Do we really believe that after spending a full day at school our children should be given hours of homework so they have no time to spend with their families? What are we teaching them? Is that a habit that will lead to a healthy life? Working all day and then bringing the office home at night?

When a teacher or school official reprimands our child for independent thinking and speaking their mind, what do we do? Do we stand up and support our kids or do we fold under the pressure of "supporting the school?" What does this say to kids about our commitment to them? What example does it set for them when they encounter injustice in the world?

When our child is labeled as "slow learner," "ADHD," "troublemaker," or "class clown," do we take the time to explore it with our kids or do we jump right in and reinforce the label? Maybe the "slow learner" is contemplative, like Eckhart Tolle. Perhaps the ADHD child is the next Steve Jobs. Is the troublemaker really a problem child or just stuck in a system that fails to motivate her? Who says the "class clown" isn't the next Adam Sandler-in-training?

And the biggest questions of all:

"Is it okay, ever, for us to allow a child to fail?"

"What does it say about our values that we do?"

These are the questions we as parents have an opportunity to explore with our children—searching for the answer that works for both your child and your family and then staunchly standing up for your child's right to learn in the way that best suits them. I believe this is the number one way by which we change the world. Forget about change being slow. With one generation of children who are loved, inspired, and supported in their dreams, this world would be vastly different.

With his smart-ass essay and stubborn refusal to be pushed down, my amazing son taught me this lesson. I love him deeply and admire his courage to blaze this trail and show us the way.

What is your child trying to teach you?

·23·

THE MONK AND THE BOY
IN THE BASEBALL CAP

THE OTHER DAY I WAS TAKING A WALK WITH MY FRIEND WANG BO, the Buddhist monk from the Shaolin Temple.

The first thing you need to know about walking with Wang Bo is that it isn't really walking as we know it. It's a meditation. Slow. Quiet. Deliberate.

We were walking contemplatively down the beach. Lift ... step ... place. Lift ...step ... place. Left foot then right ... lift ... step ... place. Lift ... step ... place.

A man walked by with his little boy a few feet behind him. I didn't really notice the man, but the boy caught my eye. He was small, maybe five or six. He wore a blue Los Angeles Dodgers baseball cap. And he was doing something curious.

He kept falling down. Not because he couldn't walk, but because he wanted to fall. He'd walk a few steps and then all of a sudden he would fall with a silent thud into the sand. Then he'd yell "OUCH!" His dad would say something like, "Get up." Then the boy sprang to his feet with his hands raised in the air like an Olympic runner winning the gold. He kept doing this ... over and over ... until I couldn't see him any more.

The second thing about walking with Wang Bo is he doesn't talk much. It's a quiet, plodding walk. Every once in a while a smile, a pat on the back, and a question. The questions are not of the normal "How ya doin'?" type. They are more like, "Jason, what do you think the birds are thinking?" or, "What's more important in life: love or health?" I guess they're the kind of questions you would expect from a monk.

On this day, after we passed the boy and his father, Wang Bo asked me, "Did you see that boy?"

"Yes," I said. "Funny."

"Why do you think he kept falling down like that?" Wang Bo asked me with the twinkle of a teacher about to teach a lesson.

I had been thinking the same thing when I saw the boy. From far away I thought maybe he was challenged in some way. Up close, it was obvious he was just having fun. But the question Wang Bo was asking me was deeper. I contemplated while we walked.

Lift ... step ... place ... lift ... step ... place ... .

Lift ... step ... place ... lift ... step ... place ... .

"I think he wanted to experience himself," I said after a bit. "He was walking with his dad. At first that was probably nice, spending quiet time with his father. But then I bet he got bored. So he fell. When he did he felt the pain ... and the excitement of hitting the sand. Then he got attention from his dad when told to get up. He experienced triumph and raised his hands."

"Hmm," Wang Bo responded. "Just like life."

That was the end of the conversation between us. Still, the question had a life of its own. Wang Bo knew this when he asked me. The question floated like a butterfly in my mind for the rest of the day. Fluttering around, a thought here, a thought there. Back and forth until the question became an answer.

You see, there is an aspect of the problems in our lives that we often overlook. Sometimes when we can't fix an issue in our lives it's because there is something else going on. At times we can't solve our problems no matter what we do because we're getting such a pay-off from them that deep down we don't really want to solve them.

It's like the little boy. He knew how to walk just fine, had no problem walking when he wanted to. But he kept choosing to fall. Why? Because he was getting a reward from it. What was the reward? A break from the boredom of walking quietly, the thrill of hitting the sand, attention from his dad, the drama of jumping up and raising his hands.

For most people falling down repeatedly and hitting the ground with a THUD is a horrible option. For that little boy, though, the option of walking for another mile quietly, boring step by boring step, was so painful that choosing to fling himself to the ground was a welcome reprieve from the monotony.

We do the same thing in our lives. Our problems, our challenges, and even our sicknesses and tragedies all have mini pay-offs. Sympathy, a dozen roses, a hug from our co-workers, a kiss from our spouse, a moment of silence in a chaotic life, and on and on.

Guru Singh once asked me a similar, but more direct version of the question Wang Bo had posed. "Are you ready to live a life so wonderful that no one will ever feel sorry for you again?"

The knee-jerk reaction is to say, "Hell yeah!" But are you really?

I certainly wasn't when I was first asked the question. My life, in many ways, still revolved around the attention I got from being a single dad, overcoming the deaths of my mom and grandma, the grind to make it, and all the smaller life dramas I exploited with a little innocent guilt.

Yet I dreamed of a great life, filled with love, success, spiritual realization, expansion, etc. Where was the disconnect?

The answer was, like most of the things we have trouble explaining, my programming.

I had been taught from the very earliest age that the number one, surefire way to get attention was for someone else to see how amazingly hard my life was and give me a giant, "Oh my God, how do you do it, Jason?!"

Right? Isn't some part of you smiling a sneaky little "I just got caught" smile? Don't you see some aspect of your life that you say you want to change but haven't been able to … and now you see why?

That's the pay-off.

A few months after Guru Singh asked me if I was ready, I told him I was. "Great," he said.

Uh oh. Just like I was explaining above about Wang Bo, the way his lessons aren't quite as simple as they seem, the same is doubly true for Guru Singh. That is, when he said "great" I should have known there was more to come.

A few weeks later, Guru Singh introduced me to another of his students who was leaving a session while I was going in. The intro went something like, "This is Jason. He has an amazing, easy life blessed with money, an amazing wife, perfect children, and a deep understanding of himself. This is the luckiest guy I know."

What did I say? You guessed it. "Well, I wouldn't say lucky-EST. It took hard work to get here. And raising the kids was a challenge, but you know...." Feel sorry for me yet? Neither did Guru Singh. He winked at me as if to say, "Are you sure you're ready?"

All of those things are true. I did work hard. Raising the kids was a challenge. Many things in my life didn't go exactly the way I planned. And the giant question I asked myself was, "So what, Jason? Do you want to be happy? Or do you want to focus on the struggle?"

Because had I continued to focus on the struggle it took to get "here," I would have continued to attract more struggle. As we've learned, our brains are masters at this. The brain will find a way to get for us what we are focused on.

I took inventory of the tactics I used to feel loved and appreciated. My favorite ploys: sympathy and guilt. I made a mental note of the questions and situations that triggered the sympathy card and I consciously replaced them with new positive answers that reflected the me I wanted to be.

Here are some of my examples:

Question: How are you?

Old answer: *I'm okay. You know, hangin' in there.*

New answer: *Wonderful.*

Question: Wasn't that hard?

Old answer: *Yeah, you know how it goes. Gotta push through a pile of shit to get to something good. It turned out okay, I was hoping for more, but it coulda been worse.*

New answer: *It was a great learning experience. Pushed me to the limits and showed me what I'm made of. And it all worked out like I knew it would.*

Question: Are your kids always this well behaved?

Old answer: *Are you kidding? They drive me nuts most days. They're putting their best feet forward showing off for you.*

New answer: *I love them through all their expressions and stages. We are growing and learning together as a family.*

Question: You're so lucky. How did you find a woman like that?

Old answer: *Hey you know, man. They're all crazy. Just gotta take the good with the bad.*

New answer: *She sure is. I just kept thinking of the type of woman I* *wanted to spend my life with and one day there she was!*

You might ask, "What if it's not true? What if my life sucks and my wife is crazy and my kids are a pain in the ass?" That's a fair question and one I asked as well.

I had problems in my life just like all of us. In fact, there is a version of my life that was horrible—no dad, my mom died, two divorces, I was a single father, and I lost my job. All that is true. But when I used those problems to get sympathy from others, I was destined to see my life as a pathetic mess. Even though I hated how pathetic I felt, I found it surprisingly difficult to give up the reward of all the attention I got for having that sad story.

Once I kicked my addiction to sympathy, I chose to tell a different story—a lifetime of great mentors, my mom showing me a path to love as her dying gift, finding my soul mate, wonderful children, the freedom to learn from amazing teachers around the world and share it through this book. I wasn't painting a turd and calling it a cupcake. I was allowing the situation to be as it is, turning down the volume on the challenging parts of my life and instead focusing on the positives. That's how I finally released my tired old story and as a result gained a lesson in both life and food.

It's so much nicer to quietly eat a cupcake ... a gluten-free, naturally sweetened, organic cupcake ... than to eat turd after turd for the rest of our lives and tell people how shitty it is.

·24·

BACON-WRAPPED HOT DOGS

NOT LONG AGO, MY WIFE AND I SPENT SOME TIME WITH GRANDMA AGGIE (Agnes Pilgrim). At age 89 she is the oldest living member of the Takelma tribe of Native Americans and the chairperson of the International Council of 13 Indigenous Grandmothers—a group of indigenous leaders from around the world who are working to improve the world through the unity of their traditions and beliefs.

Before meeting Grandma Aggie I expected her to be a frail, quiet, demure woman with a long robe and moccasins. Instead, I was face to face with a feisty, stubborn woman in a golf cart hollering orders through a megaphone. She was more Thelma Harper from *Mama's Family* than Pocahontas. She's a grandma, but she's also the tribal leader and knows how to get respect.

I overheard a conversation between Grandma Aggie and a reporter that stuck with me. Grandma Aggie was explaining the connection between all humans and nature. She told the reporter that this connection is the beauty of the world.

The reporter responded with a logical question: "So what do you do when you encounter ugly in the world?"

Grandma Aggie, with the stubborn knowing that is her hallmark, replied, "Young lady, there is no ugly. Haven't you been listening to anything I've been saying? It's all beautiful. The whole world is one— you, me, the trees, the river, the salmon—everything is one. And it is all beautiful."

I was pondering those words one day as I went for a walk from my house to the beach. How could such a strong woman whose ancestors had been slaughtered, their land confiscated, and their values trampled see only beauty in the world? How could she believe that we are all one?

I walked by a memorial outside my neighborhood firehouse. I'd seen it many times. It's a large piece of a charred steel beam taken from the rubble of the World Trade Center. Written on the stone column that supports the beam are the words "9-11-2001, Never Forget."

I understand the intent behind this memorial. I know the city and firefighters who built it meant well. They wanted to remember their fallen brothers, the brave men and women who rushed into the burning towers to save others. They wanted us never to forget the heroes.

For a moment, though, let's put aside the intent. Let's think about what this memorial really says. What feelings it truly provokes. I'll tell you what I feel. Every time I walk by and see the burned steel I remember the terrifying image of those planes flying into the World Trade Center. I remember people running for their lives down New York streets as the buildings collapsed. I remember all the people I knew in New York who were in a state of panic. And I get pissed. I want revenge.

"Good," some people say. "That will keep this kind of savage attack from ever happening again."

But is that true? Haven't we actually seen the exact opposite happen?

I remember the first few weeks following the attack. Do you recall? Americans united, standing together. Remember the feeling? The love you had for your neighbor? The newfound respect for police and firefighters? We gave money in record numbers, forgetting about our own physical needs to help others. This was the concept of "we are all one" demonstrated before our very eyes. Hell, we even liked George Bush for awhile. Remember him standing with a bullhorn on top of the rubble inspiring us and the world?

Then something changed. What was it? We like to blame it on Bush or Congress or Halliburton. But that's not fair and to believe it misses the subtle truth, the lesson in all of this.

We stopped focusing on the moment. We left the NOW. The event shocked us, took us out of our programmed lives. It made us forget our individual needs and instead focus on the larger community. In an instant those planes brought us into the present moment. In the present only love exists, the same love that Grandma Aggie sees.

Then just as quickly we snapped out of the NOW and our subconscious took over. Programmed with fear and a belief that everything good has come through great struggle and sacrifice and violence, we retreated back to our animal instincts of survival. We rallied together not to rebuild, but to retaliate.

In short, we went from seeing love to seeing only hate.

Then what happened? We went to war. Not one but multiple wars. Wars that rage on today. Wars that show no sign of ending, perhaps ever.

We have manifested those words on the firehouse "Never Forget." But instead of remembering the love and heroism, we remember the anger, hate, and death of an ever-increasing number of young men and women, Americans, Iraqis, Afghanistanis, moms and dads, sons and daughters. We don't need a memorial of charred steel. We have a real-life reminder playing out each day, transmitted on the Internet and on the nightly news.

This isn't new. This is our history. Like my family story passed from my grandma to my mom to me. We have a national story, passed from one warring generation to the next to the next and on and on.

I remember taking a trip to Hawaii when I was in seventh grade. My mom was dating a NASA pilot. He was sent to Hawaii to do some work and somehow, with his help, we were able to go with him. It's where my love for the ocean began. Not because of the ocean itself, but because of the effect it had on my mom. She was relaxed, like all the fear melted away with each ebb and flow of the ocean tide. I also learned something else on this trip.

In order to get time off from school, I received assignments from each of my teachers. My history assignment was to visit the *USS Arizona* memorial and to write about the experience. Standing on the ferry, straining to get a glimpse of the ocean memorial, I had an experience I'll never forget.

I was surrounded by older, white men. Many were wearing shirts or hats emblazoned with logos of their military division. They were World War II veterans who had come to remember their fallen friends. Mixed into the crowd, shorter and not as noticeable to me, were many Japanese tourists. They also had come to remember and were busy snapping pictures and talking amongst themselves. I was too young to realize this was a recipe for disaster until a tall, elderly white man pushed one of the Japanese tourists and yelled, "You Japs did this. Now get out of the way and let us remember in peace."

I empathize with the pain the man must have felt. Recalling the fear of war, the pain of loss, and then having to share the space with someone he was taught was his enemy.

But the truth was, and is, that the Japanese tourist wasn't his enemy any more than I was. He was just a man. Maybe inside he was feeling the same rage. Maybe his brother or father was buried under the sea, or back at home in an unmarked grave. Just like the hunk of steel outside the firehouse, this memorial of death was provoking thoughts of fear, rage, and revenge.

When I was in fifth grade I had a teacher's aide. I can't remember her name, but I will always remember her face. She was an older Japanese woman whose kind eyes and warm smile lit up my young heart. I never thought about where she had come from, only that she was there for me. On August 6 that year, I learned her story. She had grown up in Hiroshima. On August 6, 1945 she and her older sister went to school like all little children around the world. The difference that day was that a bomb was coming their way. A bomb dropped by American airmen in retaliation for the attack on Pearl Harbor. My teacher's aide was one of the lucky children that day. She had been sent to clean in the school's laundry room and when the air sirens began to scream she instinctively jumped in the iron cleaning tub and hid, not sure what was going on. That tub saved her life; her sister wasn't so lucky.

As an adult I always wondered what it was like for her to teach American kids about that war, the war that had taken her sister's life. How could she read us those American History books that described the tragedy of lives lost at Pearl Harbor, and then went on to describe August 6 as that great day in 1945 when we dropped the bomb that ended the war? What did it feel like for her that the history book overlooked her story and the story of her dead sister?

God bless America … what about her? And the rest of the world?

What's the point? War is bad? That's too simplistic. The real question is, why do we celebrate it? Why do we confuse the heroism of brave men and women with the need to memorialize death and tragedy and fear?

How different would that firehouse be with a memorial of a firefighter reaching his hand out to a small Iraqi boy? What kind of experience would we have if the *USS Arizona* memorial was a room of chalkboards where men and women, Japanese, American, and all nationalities and races, could come and write messages of peace and forgiveness? What if we took all the money we spent hoisting pieces of burnt steel outside city halls and used it to help the young men and women coming home mutilated by war; what if we used the money to build places where moms and dads who had lost their children to war could gather? What if our history books taught history from the point of view of the world in which we want to live? Instead of taking kids through the history of this country war by war, battle by battle, what if instead we focused on the innovations, the creativity, the courage to love that characterizes so many great men and women throughout history? What if we taught that America is a great country, a country in a community of great countries we call the world? And that we are citizens not just of our country, but part of a global community of people just like us—exactly like us—99.9999% the same as you and me. People who love their families, work hard to provide, and dream of all their lives can be.

I went to a baseball game the other day. It was the World Series and the San Francisco Giants were playing the Detroit Tigers. My friend Dan is a Giants' fan so I flew up to enjoy a game with him.

When the 7th inning came around attendees stood to do the traditional

7th inning stretch. "God Bless America" was performed by a military bugler. It was a touching moment. Everyone took off their hats and lowered their heads. Those who didn't were reprimanded sternly by the seriously patriotic men showing their level of their love for our country. We were told to remember the men and women fighting for our freedom around the world, and then … .

… Then we starting singing "Take Me Out To The Ball Game." Just like that. From war and fallen soldiers to peanuts and Cracker Jacks, and then back to the ballgame.

At the end of the game we meandered out of the stadium along with the other 50,000 fans. On the sidewalks surrounding the stadium were vendors hawking blankets and jackets and hot dogs wrapped in bacon. Sitting alongside them were men in wheelchairs, signs identifying them as veterans, down on their luck looking for some help.

Here we were. The same 50,000 people who had removed our hats, lowered our heads, remembered the men and women fighting around the world, and then sang in unison "God Bless America." Did each of us reach into our pocket and help out the very people we had been singing about an hour earlier?

Nope. More people dropped seven dollars for a bacon-wrapped hot dog on their way out than bothering to drop even a few quarters into the veterans' hats. If we're honest, those who did probably had thoughts like, "He better use that change to buy some food and not waste it getting loaded on beer."

Kind of like the three beers we all had watching the game? But that's different. Right?

You see, it's not that we're mean or bad or don't care. It's that we get so caught up in what we think we're supposed to be doing—working, singing "God Bless America," rushing out of the ballpark to get home, building a memorial, remembering a tragedy—that we don't take the time to stop and feel. We forget what Grandma Aggie said, that we are all one.

Not one of us, if we took the time to put ourselves in the place of the disabled veteran, legs blown off in a war he was told to fight, looking for a meal and a smile, would callously buy a bacon-wrapped weenie and walk on by. That's just not who we are as a people. But we do it because we're in a rush to get to the next thing, because no one has given us a gold star in life for taking the time to feel.

We keep ourselves feeling productive by staying endlessly busy building things like memorials. We pause long enough to remember to give a speech. Then we jump back on the hamster wheel and buy a hot dog on the way out of the game because we won't have time to eat before fighting traffic to get to the next meeting we need to attend, to plan where we're going to build the next memorial ... this is exhausting! And I'm not pointing fingers. My hamster wheel was whirring at a dizzying clip for most of my life.

Here's another possibility. Let's take just a moment to breathe ... to observe, feel, take it in, and consider that every individual and circumstance has a unique viewpoint. Every one of us sees things through the bias of our life experience. We are all doing our best given our version of the world. But there is a place where we're all the same ... where we can find compassion and understanding for everything. In order to access it, we have to turn down the volume of our programmed brain's ramblings and instead listen from our hearts.

Just like my sweet Japanese teacher's aide and just like Grandma Aggie, two women with every justification to hate America and Americans. Instead, they both look beyond the fear and anger of their childhoods, they find the NOW, and they center themselves in the oneness of us all.

In doing so they remind us of the true beauty that lives in our hearts. That makes them the greatest memorial of all.

·25·

OLD FRIENDS, A HEALTHY MEAL, AND A GOOD BOOK

THE OTHER DAY MY FRIEND, MANUEL, SENT ME A SIMPLE TEXT. "I NEED to see my friend."

I have known Manuel for 15 years. We have shared lots of memories and lots of wild adventures. You know the things that young men in their twenties and thirties do. We've all seen the movie *Hangover*. The first one, not the second one with the REALLY crazy Bangkok scenes.

When I started to make changes in my life, suddenly my days were filled with new activities—therapy to show me my core, discipline to stay there, no more alcohol, a vegetarian, high-nutrient diet, yoga, and meditation. I also stopped seeing many of my friends. We just didn't seem to have much in common anymore. I had settled into my new life, in my house, with my wife and my kids and a few good books. I ventured out to visit my teachers and then returned to my sanctuary. I surrounded myself with people and things that supported my new lifestyle.

Months went by, then a year, then two. I didn't really see any of my old friends. Every once in a while I would get a text or a voicemail, but no real connection.

Until now. Until Manuel's simple words, "I need to see my friend." So we scheduled a dinner at my house for the following Friday.

Then the emotions came sweeping in with their taunting voices:

Guilt. "You've abandoned your friends. That's not very compassionate or enlightened."

Fear. "He's probably going to think that you're a weirdo—vegetarian, meditation, yoga."

Insecurity. "Who are you to be living like this and writing a book? Manuel knows the real you, and that's nothing like this new Jason."

Then it hit me. Manuel didn't know the real me. What he knew, what we all knew, were stories.

For men, those stories aren't usually very deep. In fact, they're like those short, simple stories we're taught as little kids.

When I was going from fifth to sixth grade, my school had a summer reading challenge. Anyone who read 15 books over summer vacation would start the new school year with an ice cream party. This was my chance to get that ice cream party I had missed out on the day I was sick, remember? So I quickly signed up for the challenge and then left for summer break.

The only problem was, I didn't really want to spend my summer reading. I wanted to play baseball and football and lie around and do absolutely nothing. So I did. In fact, I never thought once about that reading challenge until my mom reminded me that school was starting up again in two weeks.

Two weeks? Oh crap. How could I possibly read 15 books in two weeks? I rode my bicycle to the library and started to look around. *The Hobbit*, nope too long. *Mouse and the Motorcycle*, too many pages. *The Lion, the Witch and the Wardrobe* ... way too long. Then I saw a group of little children sitting around a really old lady with blue hair. You know how hair starts to turn bluish with old age? Well, there they were, 20 or so little kids sitting in a half-circle in front of the blue-haired lady and she was reading: "See Spot run ... see Spot sit ... see Spot lie ... ."

So I read not 15, but 20 books that summer. I read them all in two weeks, but no one knew that. They were all simple, little, gold-bound children's books with pictures of dogs and cats and stick people on the covers. No one knew that either because all anyone at the school did was check to see if the paper was full and that you had signed your name.

That's what the stories among men are like. What we call a relationship is really a series of short, simple stories strung together into an, "I like that guy, he's all right, man."

Think I'm nuts? Try out the next paragraph.

See–Spot–run ... how's–the–game? ... see–Spot–sit ... check out–that–chick ... hear-Spot-bark ... wanna–'nother–beer? ... see–Spot–play ... how–is–work? ... see–Spot–fetch ... it's–just–fine... .

Sound familiar? Women tell epic stories, sweeping dramatic novellas compared to men. We men have short, nothing-too-deep-or-emotional, practical conversations that we call a relationship.

As I got real with myself, as I went from practical, go–to–work …
stay–there–late … try–to–get–paid … to a truer understanding of myself
and my world, it made sense that I had distanced myself from my friends
and the old stories.

The truth is, that was hard. And lonely. Because we all want to belong.
We all want to be part of a group. Even if that support is the emotional
equivalent of a stick figure and a doggie, it doesn't matter.

Deep in our DNA is an instinctual need to stay with the herd. To never
stray too far out. Why? Because in our DNA is the programming that
the animal straying from the herd dies. It gets eaten by something bigger,
stronger, and meaner. That's why making change is so hard. Our DNA is
desperate to keep us where we are, fitting in, the same as everyone else.

However, I had hope. Manuel's text was different. "I need to see my
friend" is about as raw and deep as we men get with each other. Maybe
this get-together would be a real connection, a chance to share what I had
learned over the last few years, an opportunity to get to really know my
friend at the same time.

Friday night rolled around and the doorbell rang. Manuel and I
exchanged hugs. I introduced him to Christy and showed him around my
house. Then we sat down.

"It's great to see you," I said.

"Yeah, me too," he said. "I was kind of waiting for you to reach out.
Wanted to give you your space. Then I just decided I really missed my

friend and so here I am ... ."

Hmm, this doesn't sound like see–Spot–run, I thought.

He continued: "I know you've done a lot of work on yourself. Understanding stuff, things we don't usually talk about. Your mom, your relationships, your feelings, and, well ... I really just wanted to hear what you've learned. See how maybe I might use it to find some of the peace I hear you've found."

I couldn't believe it. What was happening?

We spent the next two hours talking. Maybe for the first time in our friendship, truly connecting. Laughing, not superficially, but laughing at the common threads of our lives and the themes that recurred for us both. Good, juicy, real conversation. The kind you feel really good about. A talk from which two people learn and grow.

As Manuel was leaving he said, "I really needed this. Thank you for sharing."

I spent the rest of the night and part of the next day sorting through what had happened. I came to the conclusion that we're all searching, in our own ways, for the same things. When we get together, watch the football game and have a beer, it's not really about watching a bunch of men run around and smash into each other. It's just a safe way of connecting. A way to feel connected without any risk.

What happened that night with Manuel was the same thing. Only there were no helmets, shoulder pads, or warm beers. There was safety, except this safety opened the door for more than cheering. It was an inviting environment where two people could share their lives, fears, insecurities, hopes, and dreams without being laughed at, or made the butt of someone's joke.

Beginning with Manuel's courage to reach out, to take the step to say, "I need to see my friend," we had rewritten the rules. We told a new story that, deep down, we both wanted to tell but didn't know how.

I think it's the same for us all.

My house became *that* house. No longer the place to come and have a few too many drinks, but instead to come by for a healthy meal and a meaningful conversation and leave with a good book and big hug.

Soon my friends, all of them, started coming by one by one after hearing about my new life.

It was, and is, truly beautiful; a new life, the one I dreamed of deep in my core. Just as I learned on that walk on the beach, with my mom's memory and the dolphin, I only had to look up—or in this case, open up—to find that I wasn't alone.

·26·

SALTY MUFFINS, THE PLUMBER, AND THE PATH TO GOD

MANY YEARS AGO, I WAS REALLY CRAVING CORNBREAD. I FIGURED IT couldn't be that hard to make. Seriously, those box mixes are easy enough for kids to make, right? I bought a box of instant cornbread mix, added some special ingredients to make it my own, and put them in the oven. (Note to self: the reason it comes in a box with clear, kindergarten-like instructions is so men don't mess it up by making it "their own.")

When the timer went off, I couldn't wait to try them. I flipped over the pan and my muffins sat steaming on the counter. I knew they were too hot, but since I really wanted to eat one I did that thing my mom taught me and I blew on one to help cool it down.

After blowing and blowing on that muffin, I popped it in my mouth. And ...UGGHHHHHHH. It was frickin' horrible. Apparently my "special ingredients" had included too much salt. In fact all I could taste was salt.

I did what any man in my position would do: I hid the evidence. I crammed them down the garbage disposal, all thirteen of them, because I was a baker, and thirteen makes a baker's dozen. Then I turned on the water and the garbage disposal, and ... grrrrrrrrrrrrr ... grrrrrrrrrrrrrr

... come on baby you can do it ... grrrrrrrrrrrrr .... And as the garbage disposal desperately tried to move my thirteen salty muffins through the pipes, the water in the sink started to rise ... and rise ... and rise.

I lived in an apartment at the time, so I called the superintendent and he came right over. Have you ever noticed how all supers look like Schneider from *One Day at a Time*—mustache, white T-shirt, and jeans that don't quite cover up the butt?

So in walked the super with a bucket in one hand and a wrench in the other. He set the bucket down by the door and crossed to the sink of my small apartment. Then he did what plumbers always do, he tapped on the pipe. Then he tapped a few more times with a bit more force, as if his wrench were a magic wand that would instantly clear up the problem.

It turned out that the wrench was, well, a wrench. And I guess the super was a little stronger than he thought. When he tapped on that pipe it burst and water went spraying everywhere. I mean everywhere. My kitchen sink turned into Old Faithful and there, trapped in his own mind, stood the super, one hand holding the wrench and one hand reaching for the bucket still sitting by the front door. In that split second, he couldn't decide what to do, fix the pipe with the wrench or run for the bucket. Doing neither, he just stood there...paralyzed ... while water gushed onto the floor of my apartment.

That, in one embarrassingly true story, is the state of spirituality in our society today. We, like the plumber, stand paralyzed, stuck between old traditions and theology on the one hand and the real-life issues we confront in our daily lives on the other.

We debate whose version of God is right and whose is wrong while the world drowns in the muck of not thirteen, but seven billion salty muffins.

We spend billions of dollars fighting disease and obsessing about the perfect diet to lose weight all the while eating and drinking ourselves into sickness and obesity, walking past the simple solutions that live in the produce aisle.

We work to make money to get the things we want, only to be so stressed out and exhausted by our debt that we never enjoy what we have.

We raise our children based on someone else's rules, timelines, and priorities and then wonder why kids rebel and look for safety outside the home.

Most importantly, we talk endlessly about fixing the world, about helping the poor, cleaning the rivers, saving the whales, and we never ask ourselves the question, "Who is caring for me?" We miss the paradox that a pure world cannot come from a sick and unloved people.

We are so caught up in our stories of right and wrong that we have forgotten what life is all about. We are so concerned with being right, frantically seeking the satisfaction that comes with being told "you got it baby, gold star, off to heaven you go," that we miss the whole point of this life ... to love ourselves and others.

My journey started with two simple and yet impossibly complex questions: "Who am I?" and "Who is God?" After all the searching I have come to believe that the answer is simple and the same for both – LOVE. It's such an easy answer and yet we make it so difficult.

Starting as little children we learn that it's a dangerous, complex world. We're taught all the things to do to be "good" and all the things that are "bad." This becomes our programming. Then we layer on religious theory and a judgmental caricature of God and by the time we arrive at adulthood we have spent so many years looking through this filter that we can't see the truth in front of our faces; or better stated, in our hearts.

If you believe that to gain God's grace you have to get down on one knee and accept Jesus as your Lord and Savior, do it; then get on with truly loving yourself and all your neighbors.

If you believe that God shines within while you're meditating in lotus position, then nail your butt to the floor and boldly share your light with the world.

If you find God while communing with nature, don't stop at hugging the tree; hug yourself and then hug your children.

If you worship your job, then right from your executive chair, use your position to find joy in life and better the lives of those who work for you and with you.

And if money is your god, by all means go make a lot of it and use it to create the life of your dreams; then spread it around to those in need.

This is Heaven on Earth, the Kingdom of God in real time. Our greatest issue isn't where we will go when we die; it's what are we doing right now, while we live. When we die we'll all find out what happens. In the meantime, why not spend the precious moments of our lives focused on living the best version of ourselves that we can, a life centered around joy and love?

If we fight in the name of God, if we kill and hate and judge and discriminate and we make God into the spiritual equivalent of the Hatfields and McCoys, then what good is God? Really. Think about it. Do we really need that God?

Once, in the middle of a painful breakup, I asked Guru Singh what my responsibilities were. He told me simply, "Cause no harm. Look for the similarities. Find yourself in the other."

This may sound like spiritual nonsense, but it's a belief that has served me well. If we start from our similarities, and not our differences, what will we find?

We all live on the same planet together; we are mothers and fathers, brothers and sisters, sons and daughters. We all want the best for our families. We dream. We strive. We have fears that we overcome some days and others not. Deep down, deep inside, beyond all the stories and extraneous bullshit ... we all just want to be loved.

If we stop right there, if we don't go another step, what do we have?

Everything.

Because that one similarity, our desire to be loved, is greater than all our differences. Stopping at love, seeing that we are all the same, regardless of who we think we are ... to me that unity is the most beautiful definition of God.

I have come full circle in my quest to know myself and God. All the searching, the fighting, the debates, the modalities, all ending up here with this one simple truth:

WE ARE GOD

Not me or you or any one person or being, but all of us together. Born individually as a speck of God, expressing, through our individual life story, a unique perspective of our unity.

Without every other living creature, how could we ever understand ourselves? If the only thing in the world was you, how could you know yourself? What would you see? How would you describe yourself? If there was no contrast, how would you know all the subtle feelings and qualities we call life? You wouldn't. Our diversity, our uniqueness, is the perfection we all have been seeking. We can't find it in separateness because it's the product of all of us and everything as one.

That is the gift that each of us brings. I help you know yourself. You help me know me. Just as the rose shows us graceful beauty and the weed stubborn adaptability. We are connected through this never-ending chain of perspectives. All the perceived good and bad and beautiful and ugly and happy and sad exists only to show us the other. Visible for the purpose of showing God itself, to show you to me and me to you.

Who would have thought it? All that from thirteen salty muffins crammed down a drain. But that's life. The muffins were simply a story. In fact, all of life is a story. The meaning comes from how I choose to interpret the people and events that I run into along the way. I experience salty so I can later know the joy of sweet cornbread. A funny story so I can know humor in a time of pain. A poignant lesson so I can know, truly *know* in a life of searching, that God has been right here all along.

Now here I am, looking out into the world, the same world I have seen since childhood. Only instead of seeing the scary, lonely world I saw through the dark, colored lens of my family story, all I see now is limitless love staring back at me.

Drop by drop, the lessons of all my great teachers have slowly been clarifying the color of my life. Each new lesson lightening the dark swirls of color that had tinted my life since the womb, filling me with the white paint of innocence that allows me to see the simple truth.

For the first time I am seeing the world for myself, no longer through the filter of anyone's story. Just like Vera, and Guru Singh, and the Shaolin monks, and feisty old Grandma Aggie—all I can see is beauty.

It was all worth it; in fact it was perfect. My life, with all its ups and downs, all its different colors, has led me here ... to God, to the truth in me, and in you, and in us all.

... And I breathe, now truly home.

HUGS OF GRATITUDE

I WROTE THIS BOOK AS A TRIBUTE TO MY MOM AND ALL THE GENEROUS teachers and mentors with whom I have been blessed throughout my life.

There are, however, a few people I did not talk much about in the book whom I want to acknowledge here:

My sister Onne, who has shared this journey with me: your daily texts of, "I love you Bubba," brighten my days and remind me I am loved.

My nephew Ian and the bright, creative star that burns inside you … even when you don't recognize it.

My nephew Blake, who carries the loving soul and energy of my mom with such grace and wisdom.

Gonzalo, Amalia, Patti and Rudy, who make our home and our lives run with ease and joy.

Christa Bourg, for the initial edit of this book and for helping me see the perfection of the unconventional.

Kathleen Yasas, for the final edit, but so much more significantly for finding, caring for, and living the message of this book.

Jane Incao, for her love and care in the design of this book and of all of our projects.

Sharon Gitzen and Marie McGee, for allowing me to peek into your hearts and discover the love you shared with my mom.

Bruce Lipton and Margaret Horton, for showing us what a loving husband and wife look like as you live your eternal honeymoon.

Deva Premal and Miten, for the long hugs and perfectly-played notes of friendship and love.

Guruperkarma, for your grace, wisdom, and deep love—the traits of a true teacher, and a mom.

"Doc Holliday," because without him Wyatt Earp would never have truly known himself. Sometimes the bond of brotherhood is established at the O.K. Corral and sometimes your brother walks into your office in a suit, with a handful of notes and a heart of gold and your life is never the same. Your story is not directly told in this book, but it is forever etched in my heart and told every moment of every day as your influence on my life speaks through the man I am.

My wife and my children, for holding my heart with such love and tenderness. You are my greatest teachers, my treasured students, and my best friends.

And finally, to you, for reading this book and for joining me on this journey.

Big hugs of loving gratitude,